The North Yorkshire Moors Railway

THE NORTH YORKSHIRE MOORS RAILWAY

Michael A Vanns

Pen & Sword
TRANSPORT

First published in Great Britain in 2017 by
Pen & Sword Transport
An imprint of Pen & Sword Books Ltd
47 Church Street
Barnsley
South Yorkshire
S70 2AS

ISBN 9781473892088

Typeset by Milepost 92½
Printed and bound in India by Replika Press Pvt. Ltd

Typeset in Palatino

Pen & Sword Books Ltd incorporates the imprints of Pen & Sword
Archaeology, Atlas, Aviation, Battleground, Discovery, Family History,
History, Maritime, Military, Naval, Politics, Railways, Select, Social
History, Transport, True Crime, and Claymore Press, Frontline Books,
Leo Cooper, Praetorian Press, Remember When, Seaforth Publishing
and Wharncliffe.

For a complete list of Pen and Sword titles please contact
Pen and Sword Books Limited
47 Church Street, Barnsley, South Yorkshire, S70 2AS, England
E-mail: enquiries@pen-and-sword.co.uk
Website: www.pen-and-sword.co.uk

Contents

Preface

This book in the series 'Heritage Railway Guides' has been written for all those who want to know something of the story behind one of Britain's major heritage railways. It looks at the line through the North Yorkshire Moors taken over by enthusiasts, putting it into the broader history of the companies that originally built and subsequently ran it. As a guide, it cannot examine every aspect of the railway's history, and for those who want to delve further, there is a selective bibliography. The last chapter covering the preservation years reflects the views of the author, which might not necessarily coincide with those of the people who have worked, or continue to work, for the organisations mentioned.

This book is dedicated to all those who have worked for and supported the North Yorkshire Moors Railway and kept the trains running.

Polished to perfection, North Eastern Railway Class A 2-4-2 No. 674 standing on the turntable at Whitby in the first years of the twentieth century. Sixty of this type of locomotive were built to the designs of the company's Locomotive Superintendent, T.W. Worsdell, who was in office between 1885 and 1890. (Real Photos)

The up starting signal at Goathland station, a fine example made for the North Eastern Railway (NER) by McKenzie & Holland of Worcester. It was recovered by the North Yorkshire Moors Railway (NYMR) from Barlby Crossing, Selby and erected at Goathland in 1972 and then repositioned to the location illustrated here in 1987. (Author)

Introduction

One of the most interesting aspects of creating the three books in the Heritage Railway series was trying to account for the reasons why the railways have developed in the way they have after they were taken out of British Railways ownership. Obviously there have been many factors, ranging from the physical constraints of the route to the resources available to maintain and run trains. But perhaps the fundamentals of preservation and operation, and the way these two have been balanced out over the years, have influenced the appearance of heritage railways more than any management, staffing or financial issues. Because the initial aim of the Main Line Steam Trust was the preservation of a section of main line, it could be argued that the goal for the Great Central Railway in Leicestershire has been more towards the recreation of a main line with appropriate track layouts and signalling, compared to the original aim of the North York Moors Historical Railway Trust (NYMHRT), formed in 1972, that was 'To advance the education of the public in the history and development of railway locomotion by the maintenance in working order of the historic and scenic railway line between the towns of Grosmont and Pickering.'

Although this statement has been considerably refined over the years, especially since the organisation became a 'registered museum' requiring the words 'preservation' and 'conservation' to appear in the aims of the Trust, that initial emphasis on the running of trains does help explain why many original features on the North Yorkshire Moors Railway (NYMR) have been sacrificed since 1967 to provide better facilities for passengers and the maintenance of locomotives and carriages. It helps explain why so many metal-clad sheds have been erected and why track maintenance and renewal and signalling on the line have developed in the way they have. It is also important to record that the NYMR has been run as a heritage line for longer than it was in the hands of the LNER and British Railways combined, and those businesses also had to adapt to changing circumstances. But perhaps more importantly, with the exception of the original Whitby & Pickering Railway Company, no organisation before the NYMR had to operate the line as a self-contained unit. Locomotive and carriage maintenance did not have to be carried out and stock stored permanently somewhere between Pickering and Grosmont. Civil engineering and permanent way equipment and heavy lifting gear did not have to be accommodated either, all that being brought in from elsewhere when needed. In many ways, since 1967 the NYMR has had to become a self-contained LNER. All those issues and many more have combined to make the NYMR what it is today and it makes a fascinating story.

Repatriated from Greece in 1984, restored and named *Dame Vera Lynn*, War Department 2-10-0 is on the 1 in 49 climb between Grosmont and Goathland during the summer of 1989. (Author's collection)

Early Days to Best Years

When the Whitby & Pickering Railway (W&PR) was completed in 1836, it was already old-fashioned. Since 1830 the Liverpool & Manchester Railway (L&MR) had been running trains on a double train main line, demonstrating emphatically that the future was steam powered, and within a few years (1838), an even more ambitious railway – the London & Birmingham Railway (L&BR) – would be completed, one that in the twenty-first century still remains the spine of Britain's railway network.

When it opened, horses pulled single coaches on the single track W&PR at almost the same speeds as stage coaches on the country's network of turnpike roads, whereas on the L&MR and L&BR, coaches were coupled together to form trains capable of transporting many more people than a single stage coach and they were pulled by modern steam locomotives that travelled at three or four times the speed of horses.

The W&PR had much more in common with the Stockton & Darlington Railway (S&DR) opened in 1825 than either the L&MR or L&BR. On the mainly single track S&DR, there were sections where wagons were attached to ropes to run up and down inclined planes, and other places where either horses

or primitive steam locomotives were employed to pull the trains. The W&PR never used steam engines, but the reason it shared so many other characteristics with the S&DR was due to the fact both lines were engineered by George Stephenson. The initial surveys and costings for the L&MR had also been his responsibility, but due to inaccuracies in both these areas he had been replaced. Much of the credit for the design and use of steam locomotives on that line must also be placed elsewhere, in this instance with his son, Robert Stephenson, who went on to engineer the L&BR. Nevertheless, despite his blunders, and his son's growing reputation, George Stephenson still remained throughout the 1830s the leading advocate on the great benefits railways could bring to all parts of the country. He was the man everyone turned to on all matters relating to railways and this is why the promoters of the W&PR sought his advice.

Whitby & Pickering Railway

The impetus for building a line through the North Yorkshire Moors had come from Whitby. Traditionally, that community had looked to the North Sea for its trade and prosperity, but at the beginning of the nineteenth century, the whaling and boat-building industries

The wooden bridge over the Musk Esk immediately north of Grosmont Tunnel from an engraving by G. Dodgson in 'Scenery of the Whitby & Pickering Railway', 1836. Although the railway was brand new, the artist presented the scene as a romantic landscape, the bridge depicted as though spanning the moat of the rustic castle gatehouse beyond, in reality the railway tunnel entrance. (P. Waller collection)

were in decline, which also adversely affected other trades. The days of Captain Cook's voyages of discovery in wooden ships built at Whitby were over. The town, however, was still handling sea-borne coal traffic, and conscious of the growing network of railways connecting the collieries with the sea a few miles further north-west, local businessmen, many of whom had financially supported the S&DR, were considering whether to promote their own line to join it, or to look to create a new outlet for coal traffic southwards through Pickering.

By 1831, both alternatives had attracted influential supporters based on some preliminary surveys and cost analyses, and it was at this point that an approach was made to George Stephenson for his opinion on the best option. His view was that it would not be cost effective to build a railway to establish a new north-west trading route

when it was still possible to sail from Whitby to Middlesbrough and link up with the existing railway network there. He did believe there were considerable benefits to connecting Whitby to Pickering by a railway, benefits he characteristically over-estimated. He stated that there could be a significant increase in finished goods and of raw materials such as coal, limestone and timber available to those communities along its route, leading to a reduction in the costs of these commodities. A new railway would also stimulate the development of hitherto unproductive land. Many of the same arguments were used by other railway companies in the 1830s and then again during the later 'Railway Mania' of 1845/6 to justify the building of new lines.

Stephenson estimated the projected annual income of the railway would be in the region of £13,000, mainly from mineral traffic, more than covering the costs of building the 24 mile (38.6km) line, which he confidently declared would be only £2,000 a mile.

Stephenson's advocacy of the Pickering route was crucial, and a prospectus for the W&PR was issued and funds raised for a bill to be presented for the Parliamentary Session of 1833. The plans and estimates must have

been sufficiently convincing because the W&PR gained its Royal Assent in May 1833. Stephenson was appointed engineer, delegating supervision of the construction work, which began in September of that year, to Frederick Swanwick. This young engineer was involved in many of the older man's other projects, so the translation of the broad-brush predictions into the details of actual civil engineering was left to the contractors. Very quickly construction estimates were exceeded, the costs per mile doubling, largely due to an increase in the price of iron, and the W&PR was plunged into perpetual debt.

The unforgiving topography of the moors also stretched the budget. Immediately outside of Whitby, although the River Esk was diverted to save two expensive river crossings, in the 6 miles (9.7km) between there and what later became Grosmont, the river still had to be bridged ten times. At the latter, the rocky River Musk Esk had to be crossed and a 120yds (110m) long tunnel driven through Lease Rigg hill.

Once clear of the tunnel, the river valley was regained and followed to Beck Hole, where the line parted company from it to begin a 500yds (457m) ascent to Goathland village. This was the Goathland inclined plane. Almost 2 miles (3.5km) south of the incline, the railway reached its summit and entered Fen Bog, a tract of land as treacherous as Chat Moss on the L&MR and requiring similar methods of construction to get the line through to Newton Dale. The line continued to twist and turn as it followed the natural outline of this valley, dropping rapidly down towards the site of Levisham station, at one point at a gradient of 1 in 49. Beyond there the line was straight for almost 2 miles (3.5km) but still contained within the remote dale. Then, after crossing from the east to the west side of Pickering Beck, the line once again began to

The southern portal of the original Whitby & Pickering Railway (W&PR) tunnel at Grosmont. This was one of the earliest examples of the decorative tunnel entrance, a feature that became very popular in railway architecture in the 1830s, '40s and '50s. In the early days of railway travel, many passengers were transported in open carriages, and so decorating tunnel entrances in this way was intended to reassure them of the solidity and, therefore, safety, of the structure they were about to enter. It also made a statement of the taste of the company that built them, confirming their connection and respect for the past. (Author)

Newton Dale was formed by melt water pouring southwards from receding Ice Age glaciers and cutting through the sandstone rock. The resultant winding valley does not appear to have become a natural transport corridor, the Romans building their north-south road to the west and the later main road between the Vale of Pickering and Whitby developing along the eastern ridge of the valley (maintained by a turnpike trust from 1759). The Whitby & Pickering Railway was the first permanent transport route through Newton Dale. (Author's collection)

wriggle its way southwards. Civilisation was reached at Pickering, where the beck was crossed again and the line emerged into the very different landscape of the benign Vale of Pickering.

The first public passenger service between Whitby and the Tunnel Inn (Grosmont) started on 8 June 1835, and at first the prospects appeared bright after the struggles of construction, because within twelve months it was estimated that 10,000 tons of stone quarried from Lease Rigg were carried to Whitby for forwarding to London by boat. The ceremonial opening of the whole route took place the following year on 26 May. From early morning the church bells rang out in Whitby and the brass band played to celebrate the departure of the 'trains'. As stated earlier, these were not L&MR type trains. What the local spectators witnessed were eight or nine standard horse-drawn stage coaches setting out one after the other on what might have been a turnpike trust road if it were not for the iron rails set 4ft 8½in (1.44m) apart – the standard Stephenson railway gauge. With the exception of the wheels of the coaches and the rails supported on stone blocks, the scene would have resembled a procession of coaches leaving any number of inns in York, London, or any other major English town or city. One wonders what those who had experienced a journey on the L&MR behind one of Robert Stephenson's steam locomotives, carried along faster than a horse could gallop, would have thought of that first trip between Whitby and Pickering. The abandonment of one of the coaches after it derailed at least twice would certainly have been interesting.

It was undoubtedly a novelty to glide up an inclined plane, your carriage attached to a rope whose other end was connected to a water-filled tank that descended under its own weight to provide the power to facilitate your lift. But perhaps it did not quite compare with the steam-worked inclined plane that led to the terminus of the L&MR in Liverpool which, although half the length of that at Goathland, ran through a gas-lit tunnel. Perhaps the most exhilarating part of the journey that was not replicated anywhere else on the emerging railway network was the descent from the summit of the line just south of Goathland to Pickering. On this section of the line, the horses were detached and

When the railway was laid through Newton Dale it was seen, paradoxically, as both an advance in communication and stimulus to commerce, and something that enhanced and heightened the romantic wildness and remoteness of the valley. This detail from another engraving by G. Dodgson in 'Scenery of the Whitby & Pickering Railway', 1836, deliberately emphasised the latter sentiment, by showing a family in the rain next to a decrepit cottage, having just missed the railway coach that is disappearing into the precipitous Newton Dale. (P. Waller collection)

each coach ran downhill as far as it could by gravity, its speed controlled by the guard applying his brake, until horses were once again attached for the final pull into Pickering.

For the majority of the local population, who had no experience of the L&MR, the new railway must have been an attractive novelty because in August 1836 some 4,200 people travelled along the line. Statistics like this are difficult for historians to interpret without comparisons, so as a way of trying to put this into context, in 1839, the first year of operation of the single track, but steam-powered, Midland Counties Railway (MCR) between Nottingham and Derby, (both places with much larger populations than either Whitby or Pickering) it was calculated that on average, 10,000 passengers were carried every month.

When the Whitby & Pickering Railway opened in 1836, its way of working had more in common with horse-drawn stage coaches on turnpike trust roads than the more up to date Liverpool & Manchester Railway or London & Birmingham Railway. Consequently, apart from at Pickering and Whitby, there were no other recognisable 'passenger stations' on its route. In 1836, fares were advertised between Pickering, Raindale, 'Incline Station House', Beck Hole, Tunnel Inn and Sleights Bridge. By 1838, Levisham Road had been added to the list of stops and this detail from an Edwardian postcard shows what was probably an existing building there adapted for railway use. The platform was a post-1845 addition. (Commercial postcard, author's collection)

Perhaps of more significance than the transportation of curious passengers was the establishment of new industries stimulated by the opening of the W&PR. The stone quarrying around Grosmont has already been mentioned, but when iron ore was discovered during the excavation of the tunnel there, commercial quarrying soon followed. The Whitby & Grosmont Lime Co. built lime kilns close by, and both industries helped turn the growing settlement around the Tunnel Inn into the town of Grosmont.

The York & North Midland Railway

Despite these encouraging developments the W&PR Company was never able to trade its way out of debt. The anomaly of having clauses in its original Act that both allowed and prohibited the use of steam locomotives was never resolved and this reflected an organisation both out of step with the times and lacking funds for improvements.

It was during this period of stagnation that the York & North Midland Railway (Y&NMR) entered the story. This company's line opened in 1840 between Normanton, just outside Leeds, and York, one of the links in a chain of lines that formed the first continuous railway route between London and York via Derby. The company's chairman was George Hudson, a wealthy and ambitious York draper who by the mid-1840s had acquired the unofficial title of 'The Railway King' because of his considerable influence in current railway affairs. It was Hudson who pushed for the amalgamation in 1844 of the three railway companies centred on Derby to form the Midland Railway (MR) that became one of the country's most powerful organisations.

George Stephenson had engineered both the line north of Derby and the

A 1950s view of Grosmont looking north from above the railway tunnels. Just to the right in the middle of the photograph, with the hipped roof, is the Tunnel Inn. It was a short walk from there for passengers using the initial service in 1836 of two trains daily in either direction over the entire route, with the addition of a train to and from Beck Hole each day. Given the current pronunciation of Grosmont, it is interesting to see it spelt as 'Growmond' in a timetable of 1838. The tall chimney in the background belonged to the 1870s brickworks. (Author's collection)

Rillington Junction station looking north-east on 18 April 1952, over twenty years after it had closed to passengers in 1930. It still retains the characteristic overall roof designed by G.T. Andrews and provided at many other York & North Midland Railway (Y&NMR) stations, including Whitby and Pickering. The junction to the Whitby & Pickering line was just beyond the end of the platforms. (Author's collection)

Y&NMR, and Hudson had turned to him again when seeking to push a line from York to Scarborough in 1840. Hudson also had aspirations of transforming Whitby into a holiday destination, the West Cliff area of the town on the side of the estuary where the railway station was located being ripe for new developments. Key to his vision was creating a connection between the projected Scarborough line and the W&PR. The plans for the York to Scarborough line received Parliamentary approval in 1844, and by the time the Royal Assent for the purchase of the W&PR by the Y&NMR was secured a year later on 30 June 1845, the Scarborough line was only seven days from opening to traffic, having been completed in only one year three days since gaining its Act, a breath-taking achievement. On the same day the link from Rillington Junction (just north of Malton on the Scarborough line) to

Pickering was brought into use, passenger services starting in October that year.

In February 1846, the Y&NMR started work to bring the W&PR up to the standards of the rest of its double track lines. Although the W&PR had been laid with only a single track, sufficient land had been acquired by the company for two parallel lines. Timber bridges were replaced – a fine stone arch being erected at Grosmont where a new tunnel was also excavated – and the whole route was relaid with heavier rails so it could be worked by steam locomotives. The only section where this was not possible was on the inclined plane that was retained, a new stationary steam engine at Goathland replacing the original self-acting gravity system.

The down home signal (a North Eastern Railway example) at Marishes Road station between Rillington Junction and Pickering. The station was one of three on this Y&NMR link when completed in July 1845, but soon became the only one to remain open. It closed on 8 March 1965, the month this photograph was taken, looking towards Pickering. (Author's collection)

The existing W&PR buildings there and at Levisham remained in railway use, whilst new permanent stations were established at Whitby, Grosmont, Ruswarp, Sleights and Pickering. Handsome new stone buildings and roofs that covered both platforms and track were erected at Whitby and Pickering, the main entrance to the former enhanced by a five arch portico. A stone two road engine shed was built immediately south-west of that station with a new stone goods shed on the opposite side of the line. The equivalent structures at Pickering, both south of the station, were smaller, the goods shed made of stone, and the single road engine shed of brick. Cottages for employees were also provided at various places along the line, all the new buildings and the masonry structures designed by George Townsend Andrews, the York architect who was making his mark on many railways in the north-east of England in this period. From September 1846, Pickering and Levisham were served by steam hauled trains, and then in June 1847 steam locomotives started to work in and out of Whitby station. Although anyone travelling the whole length of the line did not have to change trains, the inclined plane effectively divided the route into two separate operational sections. Nevertheless, the times of journeys between Whitby and Pickering improved from the 2hr 30min to 3 hours of horse-drawn days, to just 1hr 30min going south and 1hr 25min going north. One of the earliest timetables for the summer of 1848 shows three trains a day providing this service, with the addition of an extra southbound train from Pickering to York

A view looking north at Saltersgate at the north end of Newton Dale, with the trees of Wilden Moor to the left and Lockton High Moor and Fen Moor in the background. Although the train, heading for Levisham station, was travelling too fast for the slow shutter speed of Mr Smith's camera, the double track of the Y&NMR's 1845 improvements is well shown in this 1920s photograph. (S. Smith commercial postcard, author's collection)

A clear view through the Y&NMR double track tunnel at Grosmont from the new 1845 station there. Compared with the 'gothic folly' entrance to the single track W&PR tunnel of the previous decade (hidden by the locomotive), the new tunnel relied on its massive stone blocks rather than any overt ornamentation to assure travellers of its durability. (R.N. Joanes, 20 April 1961)

Levisham station was almost 2 miles (3.5km) from Levisham village, the connecting road between the two seen sweeping out of Newton Dale in this detail from a pre-First World War postcard. Also prominent in this view is Grove House, set in a large rectangle of tree-backed ground, once the home of the Rowntree family of York. In 2016 it was for sale for £850,000. (J.W. Malton commercial postcard, author's collection)

Looking north up Park Street, Pickering, with the Y&NMR's railway station unchanged when this postcard was printed and circulated by Lilywhite Ltd in the early 1920s. Number 12 Park Street was purchased by the North Yorkshire Moors Railway (NYMR) in 1990 to provide accommodation for its head office and for volunteers. (Commercial postcard, author's collection)

A detail of a postcard posted from Whitby to West Hartlepool on 26 April 1908. It shows Sleights station on a quiet, summer day, a poster advertising Scarborough Flower Show propped up next to the entrance to the booking office. The attractive station building with its understated Tudor features and decorative, timber barge-boards, was designed by G.T. Andrews for the Y&NMR as part of that company's upgrading of the facilities on the line after 1845. (Commercial postcard, author's collection)

The new 1845 station at Pickering, like those at Rillington and Whitby, was provided with a wrought-iron, timber and slate roof that covered both platforms. It survived until 1952, two years after this photograph was taken. (Lens of Sutton Association/66383)

and two extra northbound returning services. A journey between Whitby and York could be completed in between 3hr to 3hr 15min.

All these Y&NMR improvements had been carried out during the 'Railway Mania' years of 1845/6, when hundreds of new railway projects had been floated to tempt investors. During this period of frenetic speculation, fortunes were made but many more people lost money – both small and large amounts. For others, reputations were also lost, including that of George Hudson. Having helped inflate the bubble, he suffered an investigation into his business affairs that exposed some dubious practices and led to his very public disgrace in 1849. In complete contrast, two years earlier in 1847, Robert Stephenson had become the Conservative Party's MP for Whitby, a position he held until his death in 1859.

The North Eastern Railway

Following the 'Railway Mania', there was a period of reflection and retrenchment, and eventually in 1854, as a means to secure the finances of the four railway companies serving York and the northeast, the North Eastern Railway (NER) was formed by amalgamation. One of the companies absorbed was the Y&NMR.

The line between Rillington Junction and Whitby then became a small part of the new NER's empire. The pattern of services remained the same for a few years until the inconvenience of the Goathland incline could no longer be tolerated. By the end of the 1850s it was an anachronism. In 1860 the NER drew up plans to build a new double track line from just under half a mile (805m) south of Grosmont Tunnel, where it would curve away from the old route, climbing continuously up the eastern edge of the Musk Esk valley to a point immediately above Beck Hole, in order to reach the rocky path of the Eller Beck from where this tributary would be followed to Goathland Mill. Once clear of this valley, the new route would rejoin the existing line at Moorgates, 1.25miles (2km) south of Goathland. These 'deviation' plans were approved by Parliament in 1861 and construction work started in the summer of the following year.

The whole route required some careful civil engineering not always obvious to ordinary travellers. The ledge cut for the railway immediately north of Beck Hole featured long stretches of retaining wall made up of large, beautifully dressed, stone blocks, laid at a 'batter', that is,

leaning away from the line at a slight angle so as to form a brace to the land behind the wall. The section that followed Eller Beck was particularly challenging as access for materials and space in which to drive through the line and work effectively was very restricted. The section of line on the approach to Goathland Mill was cut into the hillside above and on the east side of Eller Beck, requiring another length of stone retaining wall. The new station adjacent to Goathland Mill was perched on an impressive stone plinth, the station buildings and goods shed constructed of matching stone blocks and reached via a new bridge over the

A detail from the Railway Clearing House's map of the rail network of mainland Britain immediately after the First World War. (Author's collection)

beck. Between Grosmont and Goathland Mill the route was laid out with a ruling gradient of 1 in 49, one that George Stephenson and even his son, Robert, would have considered too steep to be worked by steam locomotives, and over the years, many trains had to be 'banked' up this incline – that is, pushed from behind by another locomotive.

The new 'deviation' came into use on 1 July 1865, finally eliminating the 1836 Goathland inclined plane. The improvement was long overdue as there had been a number of accidents on the incline, the last two both caused by the rope breaking. In October 1861 a goods train being hauled up the incline had broken free, fortunately without human injury, but then on 10 February 1864 two lives were lost with thirteen others injured, when the rope snapped on the descent of five passenger carriages.

The deviation not only improved safety, it also reduced journey times even further. The four trains serving all stations between Pickering and Whitby could complete the journey in about 1hr 10min, the two non-stop services taking only 50min. The equivalent two express trains in the opposite direction also took 50min, with the remaining four stopping trains averaging a few minutes over the hour.

After 1865, the original route between Grosmont and the foot of the incline remained open to serve the small communities at Esk Valley and Beck Hole, but southwards, tracks were removed. The incline was only used again for railway purposes very briefly during 1872 when special narrow gauge track with Fell's patent central rail was installed so that a Manning, Wardle & Co. steam locomotive destined for Brazil could be tested in June of that year.

Three months after the deviation opened, Grosmont became a junction, with the completion of a line from Picton, on the Northallerton to Stockton branch. The route had been promoted by the North Yorkshire & Cleveland Railway (NY&CR) in 1854, but had taken over ten years to reach Grosmont from the west. This was the first of four new lines built to connect with the railway between Whitby and Rillington Junction. In April 1875, a line opened connecting Pickering to Gilling via Kirby Moorside to the west, and then in May 1882, from the

The 'Goathland Deviation' of 1865 led to the erection of some impressive stone structures, including this one – bridge No. 31 – at Water Ark. The bridge crossed Eller Beck at a skew and although it cannot be seen in this Edwardian photograph, all the stones in the arch were beautifully cut at the appropriate angle and laid with very thin mortar joints. Beauty for operational requirements. (Ross of Whitby commercial postcard, author's collection)

A detail from another Edwardian postcard, this one showing the 1865 Goathland station with two very noticeable chimney stack additions indicating a recent reorganisation of the internal rooms. The design of the main station building was also used for those on the Grosmont–Castleton section of line opened in October 1865, three months after Goathland. To the right, only its roof visible through the trees, is Goathland Mill next to the wrought-iron bridge over Eller Beck. (Author's collection)

No book about the North Yorkshire Moors Railway would be complete without the reproduction of this familiar photograph. It was taken in 1893 and shows one of the NER's 'Whitby bogies' designed by locomotive superintendent, Edward Fletcher, especially for working the line after the 'Goathland Deviation' had been completed. This particular engine was posed for its portrait in front of the houses along Windsor Terrace, Whitby. (F. Moore)

In this Edwardian photograph of Goathland station, the only addition to the suite of buildings provided when it opened in 1865 was the signalbox that came into use on 1 May 1876. The prominent 'V' in the hillside behind the goods shed and station buildings marks the course of Eller Beck, descending rapidly with the railway towards Grosmont. In 1999 the NYMR converted the goods shed into a refreshment room, a very successful adaptation. (Commercial postcard, author's collection)

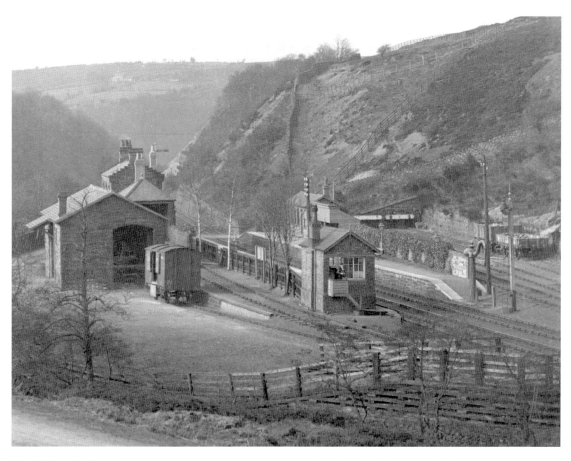

An afternoon train at Darnholm in the 1920s climbing the 1 in 49 gradient of the 1865 'Goathland Deviation' between Grosmont and Goathland. The engine is crossing bridge No. 28, its stone arch of 1865 replaced in red brick. Once preserved steam locomotives started to work this section of line again from the 1970s, Darnholm became very popular with railway photographers. (S. Smith commercial postcard, author's collection)

east, another line came in from Seamer
(the 'Forge Valley Line'), both branches
linking into the W&PR at Mill Lane just
south of Pickering station.

A few years later, Whitby was
linked to two new routes, which both
involved major civil engineering work.
In December 1883 the first to open came
in from the west, the last section of a
route originally promoted by the Whitby,
Redcar & Middlesbrough Union Railway
(WR&MUR) in the middle of the 1860s. A
new station was built in the developing
West Cliff area of the town, and then the
single track line plunged south, dropping
down Airy Hill at 1 in 50 before turning
through 180 degrees to head due north,
running parallel with the W&PR until
joining it at Bog Hill junction within sight
of the 1847 terminus.

Another signalbox brought into use in the mid 1870s to control trains on the line by
using the absolute block system, was High Mill at the north end of Pickering station.
It is seen here on the extreme left next to the engine turntable, with the masonry
remains of the thirteenth century Pickering Castle prominent in the background.
(S. Smith commercial postcard, author's collection)

The other new line, which came in
from Scarborough via Robin Hood's
Bay, opened shortly afterwards in July
1885. This line crossed the River Esk on
an impressive 13 arch brick viaduct –
Larpool Viaduct – immediately south of
Airy Hill so that the railway reached the
north bank of the river at such a height
that it could join the WR&MUR line
about half way on its descent from West
Cliff station. Inconveniently this meant
that any train to and from Scarborough
using the main terminal station in
Whitby, had to stop in West Cliff station
first to change direction.

Whitby viewed from Larpool c.1883, the single track branch promoted by the Whitby, Redcar & Middlesbrough Union Railway (WR&MUR) seen still under construction on the far left, climbing away above the W&PR double tracks. (Author's collection)

Larpool Viaduct carried the line between Scarborough and Prospect Hill Junction, Whitby, across the River Esk just south of the town. The 915ft (279m) long viaduct, 120ft (37m) at its highest point, was built as a vital part of the Scarborough & Whitby Railway between 1882 and 1884, the company retaining its independence until absorbed by the NER in 1898. The tracks of the W&PR can been seen passing underneath nearest the river, with the single line of the WR&MUR a little higher, curving sharply away to Prospect Hill and Whitby West Cliff station. (J. Chesney via R. Carpenter)

All the lines mentioned so far were not just built for the benefit of passengers but were well used by mineral and freight trains. In all parts of the country during the nineteenth century and well into the twentieth, a huge quantity and variety of items were moved by rail, as was an almost incalculable tonnage of coal of all grades used to run stationary and locomotive steam engines, feed the boilers of boats and ships and to be burnt in countless hearths heating homes, schools, shops and all sorts of other premises.

Also vital to the Victoria economy was the manufacture of iron and steel. In this the W&PR played its part by initially providing an outlet for locally produced raw materials and then later as a means of distributing semi-finished goods. Grosmont owed much of its development as a town to its lime kilns and the mining of iron ore. There were a number of mines immediately north-east of the town connected to the railway, tens of thousands of tons of iron ore extracted during the nineteenth century finding its way to furnaces in the north-east.

With the seemingly endless demand for cast-iron products during the nineteenth century, where raw materials were close at hand it was not unusual for small companies to invest in smelting their own iron, the main ingredients being iron ore, limestone and coke. Two such ironworks were established with sidings connected to the W&PR, the first built by the Whitby

A view looking due west down Front Street, Grosmont in the 1920s. The station buildings are visible above the delivery lorry, and behind that is the tall, brick chimney of the 1860s ironworks that provided so much employment in the town until the beginning of the twentieth century. (Commercial postcard, author's collection)

A photograph of NER 0-6-0 No. 659 in fully lined out, dark green livery, taken outside Whitby engine shed in the 1890s. This type of locomotive with a long boiler and oddly spaced, coupled wheels, dated back to an 1866 William Bouch design for the Stockton & Darlington Railway. A number of these old-fashioned locomotives finished their working lives at Whitby and Malton sheds. (Ken Nunn col/The Locomotive Club of Great Britain)

Iron Company Ltd at Beck Hole in 1857. Two blast furnaces for producing pig-iron from ore mined on site were erected, and in 1860 the firm cast its first iron products. Unfortunately problems forced the works to close after only a few years although mining continued a little longer.

More successful was the ironworks set up by Charles and Thomas Bagnall in 1862 to the north-west of the recently opened new railway junction at Grosmont. Two state-of-the-art blast furnaces were 'blown-in' the following year and two of the existing iron ore mines were taken over by the company.

The ironworks soon became the major employer in the town, with 500 people working there. In 1876 a third blast furnace was brought into use, the works remaining in production until 1891. For many years after that, the by-product slag was reprocessed and taken away from the site by rail, the Balcony Slag Works still being recorded in the 1956 edition of the Railway Clearing House Book of Stations.

The industry with a connection to the railway that boasted the longest life at Grosmont in its original form, however, was the brickworks established in 1870 on the opposite side of the line to the ironworks. As well as for numerous domestic buildings its hard, dark red bricks were used for some prestigious buildings such as the Roman

Catholic church of St Joseph, West Hartlepool, opened in 1895. Investment after the First World War led to the commissioning of a new Hoffman kiln in 1923, and the works remained in production until 1957.

Elsewhere on the line, building stone continued to be quarried at Lease Rigg, and the hard, dark coloured Whinstone that was used as an aggregate in road construction was quarried and mined around Goathland. These raw materials were sent out of the area by rail. The inclined plane on which the loaded narrow gauge wagons descended to sidings immediately to the east of Goathland Station, remained a prominent feature until mining ended there after the Second World War.

The limestone quarries just north of Pickering station and served by a siding running north-west behind New Bridge signalbox, remained in production until 1966.

There is little doubt the railways of Great Britain reached their zenith in the twenty years leading up to the First World War. It is fortunate that in this period hundreds of photographs were taken of railway subjects and many turned into picture postcards. Enlargements from a few are used in this book. Although these images appear to

By the end of the nineteenth century, the railways of Great Britain were the most efficient and quickest way of travelling around the country. Here, a three coach train steams purposefully away from Pickering bound for Whitby. In 1899, the early morning Mail Train would have taken just forty-nine minutes to complete that journey, an ordinary passenger a round hour. (S. Smith commercial postcard, author's collection)

show a respectable and well-managed environment, the Edwardian era and the conflict that followed marked a distinct watershed in the social and economic life of the country. There were times when the Government, industrialists and managers worried about revolution amongst workers who were increasingly prepared to strike for better pay and conditions. Yet during Edwardian summers, thousands of workers, happily and peacefully flocked to the seaside and other 'picturesque' destinations during official works holidays. Railway managers and their workforce not on holiday exploited this demand and rose to the considerable challenges of organising and operating the services.

Scarborough and Whitby had already become firmly established by the end of the nineteenth century as popular holiday destinations for both local and long distance travellers. The Great Northern Railway (GNR), for example, had been running regular through

A detail from another Edwardian photograph that was turned into a postcard. It was taken just north of Pickering. The locomotive at the front is a NER Class 38 4-4-0, built to the designs of Alexander McDonnell, company Locomotive Superintendent for a very short period between November 1882 and September 1884. Behind, is a Bogie Tank Passenger (BTP) 0-4-4T designed in 1873 by McDonnell's predecessor, Edward Fletcher, for working such branch lines as that between Rillington Junction, Pickering and Whitby. (Commercial postcard, author's collection)

The south end of Whitby station at the beginning of the twentieth century. The large roof of the goods shed can be seen on the left, with three, four-wheeled passenger carriages in front. Immediately above the signals the remains of the thirteenth century Whitby Benedictine Abbey can be seen on the skyline. (Pat Rutherford)

Another veteran NER 0-6-0, this time photographed at Malton in 1904, where locomotives were shedded for working over the Rillington Junction to Whitby route. This particular engine continued in service until 1909. (Ken Nunn col/The Locomotive Club of Great Britain)

Beckhole. Auto-Car. Station

Staff and children pose proudly next to an 'Autocar' at Beck Hole halt a few years before the outbreak of the First World War. (Author's collection)

carriages during the summer months from London Kings Cross since the end of the 1880s. Within a few years of the Great Central Railway (GCR) opening its 'London Extension' from just north of Nottingham to London Marylebone in 1899, it had put on a train to and from Scarborough as an extension of its restaurant car service between Southampton and York. As well as these services, the NER also laid on many holiday excursions from all parts of its own network of lines in Yorkshire and the north-east. In addition, during the summer of 1905, it introduced 'Autocars' between Whitby and Goathland for

day-trippers, augmented three years later using the same type of trains by services to and from a new wooden platform at Beck Hole on the original course of the W&PR. Beck Hole had long been a romantic holiday destination for the more adventurous in the area. The 'Autocars' consisted of a steam locomotive permanently attached to one or a pair of carriages, and because the train could be driven from either the engine or the rear carriage, the former did not have to be 'run around' its train at the end of each journey.

As soon as war was declared in 1914 these services and all excursions were withdrawn, to make way for trains that carried away thousands of naive volunteers as though they were going on just another form of excursion, except not to the British seaside, but to the battlefields of France. Ironically the bombardment by the German Navy of Scarborough, Whitby and Hartlepool on 16 December 1914, in which 137 people died and nearly 600 were injured, both encouraged further recruitment – 'Remember Scarborough!' becoming the new slogan – and brought home the realities of warfare to ordinary people. Under Government control from the very start of the conflict, the railways curtailed many other services so they could move vast quantities of armaments and men. As the war dragged on, further cuts were made with many stations forced to close in 1916 and 1917, and many miles of track taken up ostensibly for use in France. One of the locations where this occurred was between Pickering and Levisham, where the up (south-bound) line was recovered and single line working instigated between New Bridge and Levisham signalboxes.

A mixed goods train approaching Levisham station from the south just before the First World War, when the line between there and Pickering was still double track. The third, fourth, fifth and sixth vehicles in the train were cattle wagons, the lime used for disinfecting them clearly visible on the lower parts of their bodies. (S. Smith commercial postcard, author's collection)

Decline to Closure

By the end of the First World War, the great age of railways in Britain had passed. The story of many lines post-1918, including the route through the North Yorkshire Moors, is one of struggle exacerbated by a world-wide recession. Although the transporting of both passengers and freight over long distances remained firmly under the control of the railways, motor lorries siphoned off much local traffic, and by the start of the Second World War there were many more families who owned cars. By the 1930s, the railways to and from Whitby were only really busy during the summer months when hundreds of holiday-makers used ordinary services or took advantage of the many special excursions. During the winter months, far fewer people travelled by train. Industries along the line did not completely abandon the railway and there was even an interesting additional traffic flow created when in 1919 the Pickering Sand Co. invested in a 2.5mile (4km) long narrow gauge railway that followed Gundale Beck to connect its quarries near Saintoft Grange to the sidings at New Bridge, Pickering. The firm and the railway survived the Second World War, remaining in use until 1961.

But despite this specific resurgence, and temporary boosts in traffic due to forestry activity and its need to move timber, retaining business for the railway through the North Yorkshire Moors – both goods and passenger – became increasingly difficult between the two world wars and immediately after 1945.

The London & North Eastern Railway

In 1923, all the country's railways, with the inevitable few exceptions, were grouped into four new organisations – the NER being absorbed into the London & North Eastern Railway (LNER). The line between Whitby and Rillington Junction then became an even smaller part of a larger undertaking. Double track was never reinstated between Pickering and Levisham as the LNER considered the expenditure was not warranted. Between Whitby and Pickering in the winter months there were just five passenger trains during the week (working through to Malton), a journey stopping at all stations taking a few minutes under the hour. Sunday trains did not reappear in the timetable until the mid 1930s by which time Rillington Junction station had closed to passengers (in September 1930).

One and a half miles (2.5 kilometres) north-east of Goathland station, high up on the Whinstone Ridge on Sleights Moor, this road sign from the horse-drawn age was being seen by an increasing number of motor vehicles when this photograph was taken in the 1920s.
(Commercial postcard, author's collection)

Ten years after the Grouping of the railways, and the majority of locomotives seen at Whitby were former North Eastern Railway (NER) designs. In this 1934 photograph, London & North Eastern Railway (LNER) Class A6 4-6-2T No. 693 dominates the scene on the right, overshadowing its older stable mate, 2-4-2T LNER Class F8 No. 1581, designed in 1885 by T.W. Worsdell. The A6 class was designed by his brother, Wilson Worsdell, especially for working the Whitby to Scarborough line, and ten were constructed between 1907 and 1908. (T.E. Rounthwaite)

The south end of Pickering station on a bright summer morning in the 1920s. The crossing gates on Bridge Street are closed and the train is ready to pull away to Rillington Junction and Malton. The tracks on the left lead to the goods yard. (S. Smith commercial postcard, author's collection)

Former Hull & Barnsley Railway (H&BR) 0-6-0 LNER Class J23 No. 2453 hurries through Goathland station in June 1934 with a south-bound freight train, crossing the Eller Beck in the foreground. This J23 was one of a number of the class shedded at Whitby and Malton for working between the two places. The last two of the class were withdrawn from service at Whitby in 1938. (R. Carpenter collection)

Former NER Class O 0-4-4T, redesignated Class G5 and renumbered No. 1319 by the LNER, threading its way out of Whitby (Town) station on 1 June 1936. Class A8 4-6-2T No. 1527 is on the left and former H&BR 0-6-0 classified J23 by the LNER is on the right. Judging from its shining black paintwork, the A8 was probably not long out of Darlington Works following an overhaul, refurbished for more heavy freight haulage to and from Whitby. (T.E. Rounthwaite)

Another Class G5, this time no. 1886 hauling the 12.10pm departure from Whitby and approaching Grosmont in 1938. Despite the date, all the railway hardware that can be seen was of NER vintage: the engine, carriages, track and telegraph pole. (Real Photos)

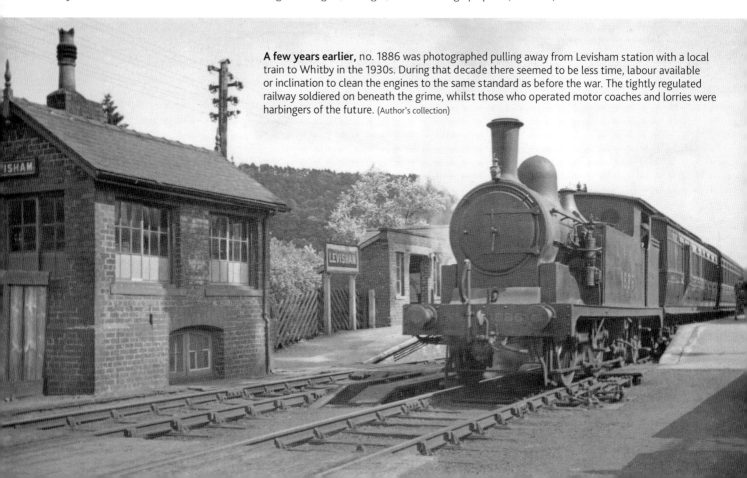

A few years earlier, no. 1886 was photographed pulling away from Levisham station with a local train to Whitby in the 1930s. During that decade there seemed to be less time, labour available or inclination to clean the engines to the same standard as before the war. The tightly regulated railway soldiered on beneath the grime, whilst those who operated motor coaches and lorries were harbingers of the future. (Author's collection)

The look and operation of Goathland station changed little after the First World War. As can be seen in this late 1930s photograph, goods trains were still well loaded, like this one hauled by a 0-6-0 LNER Class J24 and needing banking assistance on the climb from Grosmont. At the station itself, economies meant the station master was shared with Levisham, but there was still investment in local industries using the railway, as illustrated by the construction to the right of a new weighbridge office built by the LNER for the Goathland Whinstone Quarries under an agreement of June 1939. (Author's collection)

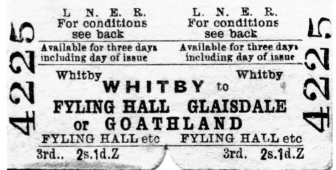

LNER tickets. (P. Waller collection)

As stated earlier, it was in the summer months when the branches to Whitby and the coast earned their money. Between Malton and Whitby, two extra weekday trains with four extras on Saturdays were added to the summer timetables. In addition, the Whitby–Goathland 'Autocar' services resumed after the war, replaced from 1932 by single carriage steam railcars built by the Sentinel Waggon Works in Shrewsbury. Each of these vehicles was given a name, many previously carried by early nineteenth century stage coaches, a practice that also recalled the earliest days on the W&PR when the horse-drawn railway coaches were named. The

Sentinels' distinctive livery of green and cream also echoed the coaching era and made them stand out against the standard teak and dark brown colouring of ordinary LNER carriages. They proved popular for both operators and passengers, and they became a familiar sight on many LNER branch lines throughout the 1930s.

The Sentinels' cheerful colour arrangement was soon applied to new excursion stock built by the LNER from 1933. The company was keen to maintain its hold on long distant summer excursions, laying on services that carried as many passengers as possible at the cheapest fares, as well prestigious ones such as the 'Northern Belle', running from Kings Cross and routed through the North Yorkshire Moors as part of a luxury 'scenic cruise' around the country. Another ploy by the LNER (and other railway companies) trying to boost their income, was the hiring

Six-cylinder Sentinel railcar No. 248, *Tantivy* being topped up with coal at Whitby in September 1938. It had a very short working life, being built at the very end of 1932 at the Sentinel Waggon Works in Shrewsbury then withdrawn immediately on the outbreak of the Second World War. Tantivy was a word describing rapid movement and was applied to a number of horse-drawn stage coaches in the previous century. In the 1830s, when travelling behind a steam engine offered faster journeys than by road, it is said stage coach drivers sang: 'Let the steam pot hiss till it's hot, Give me the speed of the Tantivy Trot.' (W. Potter)

Railcars, some steam and others petrol driven, were intended to improve the image of railway travel in the 1930s and cut down on operating costs. These vehicles were deliberately given colourful cream and light green liveries to set them apart from ordinary railway carriages and to make them as eye-catching as motor buses. Number 237 *Rodney*, seen here, was one of twenty, two-cylinder Sentinel steam railcars built in 1928 and used initially on Forge Valley services to and from Pickering. (Author's collection)

Railcar No. 2257 *Defiance* was one of twenty-eight vehicles built by Sentinel's of Shrewsbury in 1929. It was photographed with another unidentified example at Whitby, probably at the end of the 1930s. It was withdrawn at the end of the Second World War. *Defiance* was another name taken from old stage coach services, two examples once operating around Exeter, and between Glasgow and Aberdeen. (Author's collection)

Former NER 4-6-2T, LNER Class A6 No. 692 at Whitby in October 1938, its black bulk contrasting with the up-to-date motor bus on the road immediately behind. (W. Potter)

One of the innovations aimed at persuading people back to the railway in the 1930s was the fitting out of old passenger carriages as camping coaches. These were placed in sidings at a number of stations in Yorkshire, including Goathland. This snap-shot of that station sometime before the Second World War, was undoubtedly taken by the family staying in the camping coach there. The carriage roof can just be seen immediately to the right of the woman in the fashionable hat. (Author's collection)

out of camping coaches converted from redundant stock. These were parked in little used sidings at Levisham and Goathland stations as well as at other stations on neighbouring lines.

In the last years of the 1930s the country-wide economic depression was easing, but it was becoming increasingly obvious that another war was almost inevitable, and the Government was making preparations. When war with Germany was declared in 1939, the railways were immediately requisitioned and train services all over the country were severely reduced. Between Whitby and Malton the weekday timetable was reduced to just four trains each way. Whitby once again became a German target but from the air rather than the sea. One of the first enemy bombers to be shot down over the country crashed just outside the town, and in another raid a year later, the south end of the goods shed was destroyed and track uprooted. The station house at Grosmont also suffered minor damage in a later attack.

British Railways

For the first few years after the war, apart from the challenges for returning service personnel of settling back into civilian life and with rationing still in force, in locations such as the North Yorkshire Moors very little appeared to change. Nevertheless, there was an optimism that life should and would be better than in pre-war days. The obvious indicator of this perception was the landslide victory achieved by the Labour Party in the 1945 General Election. Churchill was almost universally admired for steering the country through its worst crisis for centuries, but the people wanted their say in its future, and many felt it was socialism that was going to deliver true change and not a Tory stalwart. As promised, the Labour Party nationalised the country's staple industries of coal mining and steel production; nationalised the water, gas

The LNER's October 1947 timetable as published in Bradshaw's Guide. (Author's collection)

Table 110 — MALTON and WHITBY

Miles from Malton		Week Days only						
		a.m	a.m	a.m	a.m	p.m	p.m	
103	Newcastle ..... dep	2 4	..	8 10	10 0	1 7	2 30	..
116	Leeds (City) ...	3 0	..	9 10	12 55	1 50	4 28	..
109	York	4 30	..	10 15	1 45	3 5	5 10	..
—	Malton .... dep	5 20	..	11 5	2 28	4 0	6 0	..
7½	Marishes Road	..	..	11 17	..	4 12	6 12	..
11	Pickering	5B46	..	11 27	2 45	4 20	6 19	..
17	Levisham	5 57	..	11 38	2 56	4 31	6 30	..
25½	Goathland	6 14	8 25	11 55	3 13	4 48	6 47	..
29	Grosmont	6 26	8 32	12 2	3 21	4 55	6 54	..
32½	Sleights	..	8 41	12 11	3 30	5 4	7 3	..
33¾	Ruswarp...........	Aa	8 46	12 16	3 35	5 9	7 8	..
35½	Whitby .... arr	6 40	8 50	12 21	3 39	5 13	7 12	..

Miles		Week Days only							
		a.m	a.m	a.m	a.m	p.m	p.m	p.m	
—	Whitby .... dep	7 5	7 48	9 30	1145	3 20	..	6 45	..
1½	Ruswarp............	7 10	7 53	9 35	1150	3 25	..	6 51	..
3	Sleights	7 14	7 57	9 39	1154	3 29	..	6 55	..
6½	Grosmont	7 23	8 6	9 48	12 3	3 39	..	7 4	..
9¾	Goathland...........	7 33	8 16	9 58	1213	3 49	..	7 14	..
18¼	Levisham	7 50	..	10 15	1230	4 6	..	7 31	..
24½	Pickering	8 5	..	10 29	1242	4 20	7 25	7 45	..
27¾	Marishes Road	8 11	..	..	1248	..	..	7 51	..
35¼	Malton............. arr	8 22	..	10 44	1259	4 35	7 45	8 2	..
56½	109 York........... arr	9 9	..	11 35	1 51	5 40	..	9 6	..
81½	116 Leeds (City) ...	9 55	..	12 30	2 45	6 30	..	1023	..
136½	103 Newcastle	11 3	..	2 31	3 59	9 9	..	1115	..

Aa Calls when required to set down from York.   B Arr. 5 36 a.m.   S Saturdays only.

For **OTHER TRAINS** between York and Pickering, see Table 118—Grosmont and Whitby, Table 131.

and electricity supply industries; and nationalised road haulage, waterways and the railways. In 1948, British Railways came into existence, which reduced the Whitby to Pickering line to an even smaller cog in a huge and increasingly unwieldy machine.

The people's love of the socialist experiment, however, did not last long, and in 1951 a Conservative Government was returned to power. That administration delivered road haulage back into the hands of hundreds of ambitious private owners, and as bus services expanded and car ownership increased, British Railways – still firmly in public ownership – was forced to implement the economies that the pre-

War companies knew were inevitable but had not been prepared to make. The cuts had already started before the General Election, passenger trains having stopped running over the Forge Valley Line between Pickering and Seamer from 4 June 1950. On 18 September 1951, barely a month after Churchill was returned to power, the last train on the branch to Beck Hole ran, after the former mining settlement of Esk Valley 1 mile (1.6km) south of Grosmont, previously only connected to the outside world by this line, was provided with a new road by North Riding County Council. Then from 1 February 1953 it was no longer possible to travel as a passenger by train between Pickering and Gilling via Kirby Moorside. In June the following year, passenger services between Whitby and Middlesbrough via Grosmont were modified, trains no longer running to Picton but reversing at Battersby Junction.

Putting on a show as it entered Goathland station from the north on 15 September 1950 with a long goods train, over two and a half years after nationalisation, this Class J24 0-6-0 No. 5644 was still in its LNER livery – hidden under the grime. It had, however, been fitted with a new cast shed plate – 50F – indicating that it was officially allocated to Malton motive power depot (MPD), of which Pickering was a sub-shed. It was withdrawn the year after this photograph was taken. (Author's collection)

Former LNER 4-4-0 Class D49, No. 62731 *Selkirkshire,* in the first manifestation of the new nationalised railway's livery, leaving Levisham for Pickering and Malton. The train was made up of former NER carriages. (Cecil Ord collection)

A Malton–Whitby service pulling away from Levisham station in the early 1950s behind former NER 0-4-4T, LNER Class G5 No. 67335. This locomotive was built in 1901 and lasted in service until 1953. (Cecil Ord collection)

There followed a respite of four years, then passenger services were further reduced when at the beginning of May 1958 trains stopped running between Whitby and Loftus, although West Cliff station remained open for trains to and from Scarborough until June 1961.

After that passenger trains travelling between Whitby and Scarborough changed directions at Prospect Hill Junction, Whitby, a process made easier as since 1958 diesel multiple units (DMUs) had been substituted for steam trains on this route. In 1959, DMUs also took over all but two of the five daily trains south of Whitby.

But steam haulage continued for all summer excursion traffic over the line, and through carriages from Kings Cross detached at York for Whitby still had to be attached to other steam worked trains in order to complete their journey. For this brief period in the late 1950s and early 1960s, the old and new ways of operating a railway co-existed.

Then came the Beeching Report of 1963, the result of a clinical analysis of every part of the British Railways network. The simple aim outlined in that report was to make the railways pay their way by accelerating modernisation and cutting away all unprofitable

A few pages from British Railways' 1950 'Holiday Guide' to Eastern England.
(Author's collection)

A poor photograph taken on 31 January 1953, but one that shows the signalbox at Mill Lane, Pickering, where the line from Gilling, Helmsley and Kirkby Moorside came in from the west (right) and the Forge Valley line from Seamer and Thornton Dale joined the Rillington Junction to Whitby route from the east (left). The Forge Valley line had closed to passengers in 1950, with services through Kirkby Moorside ending on 2 February 1953, a few days after this photograph was taken. (Kidderminster Railway Museum 005237)

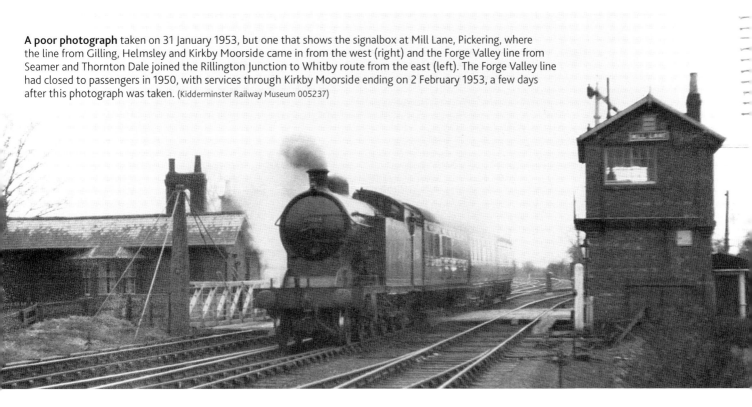

A summer holiday train from Whitby on the climb through Beck Hole with 4-6-0 Class B1 No. 61086 based at Neville Hill (Leeds) on the front and an unidentified locomotive banking at the rear. As was typical of the mid-1950s period, the engine had not been cleaned externally for many months, and all but two of the carriages of the eight coach train were former LNER teak-bodied examples, probably worse for wear after intensive war-time use. (Cecil Ord)

As local traffic disappeared from branch lines during the 1950s, summer specials between the cities of northern England and the coast became a vital source of revenue for a nationalised railway struggling to balance its books. In this photograph from the late-1950s, 0-4-4T Class G5 No. 67342 pilots 4-6-0 Class B1 around the curves at Goathland Summit with a lengthy Leeds–Whitby train. (Cecil Ord)

Holiday time at Whitby Town station in the mid-1950s. On the right, LNER 4-4-0 Class D49 No. 62731 *Selkirkshire* making another appearance and blowing off fiercely at the head of a train of former LNER teak carriages repainted in British Railways' new crimson lake and cream livery, often referred to as 'blood and custard'. In the centre road is 2-6-4T No. 80117, built at Brighton Works in 1954 and sent to Whitby shed that year. It stayed until 1958. (T.J. Edgington)

Coasting down grade on the last mile towards Grosmont with a local train from Malton, BR 2-6-4T Class 4P No. 42083 was returning to its home shed at Whitby where it was resident between October 1955 and July 1959. (Cecil Ord)

South-bound mixed goods train behind former NER Class P3 0-6-0, British Railways Class J27 No. 65888 at Darnholm on the climb towards Goathland station in the 1950s. Like the J24, this was a local engine shedded at Malton. The first P3 was turned out of Darlington Works in 1906 and the last of over 100 engines appeared in 1923 after the Grouping. This final example – No. 2392 – was withdrawn in 1967 and acquired by the North Eastern Locomotive Preservation Group (NELPG) nine years later to work on the recently formed North Yorkshire Moors Railway. (Cecil Ord collection)

activities. In North Yorkshire this meant eliminating all the remaining passenger services between Whitby, Scarborough, Middlesbrough and Pickering. The line between Middlesborough and Whitby would be retained for freight traffic as it was the one local line making the smallest loss, according to statistics gathered for the report. The same statistics claimed that the complete closure of the line between Grosmont and Rillington Junction would save almost £50,000 a year.

Beeching's plans were the most controversial in railway history and there was huge opposition to his proposals. Any objections had to be channelled through the regional Transport Users' Consultative Committees (TUCC) that were tasked with considering individual cases of hardship that might be caused by any closures. Public meetings were held in Whitby at the beginning of July 1964 at which it was stressed how important the railway was during bad winters when local roads were impassable and children had to rely on trains to get to and from Whitby schools, and what a detrimental effect withdrawal of passenger trains would have on the town's tourist trade. In August the Yorkshire TUCC made its report having received over 2,000 objections to Beeching's plans.

It seemed a strong case had been made, but the following month the Transport Minister, Ernest Marples, announced that passenger service would only be retained between Whitby and Middlesborough, and that the line south of Grosmont would be scheduled for complete closure.

With the defeat of the Conservative Party in the following month's election and the installation of a Labour administration, hopes were high that the 'Beeching Axe' might be blunted.

Looking in the opposite direction to the photograph at the top of page 51, an evening return seaside special from Whitby has more of a challenge climbing out of Grosmont on the 1 in 49 gradient. Piloting the 4-6-0 Class B1 (the train engine) was 2-6-4T Class 4P No. 42639, and as its shed plate (50F) indicates it was allocated to Malton at the time, the photograph must have been taken sometime between June 1960 and November the following year. (Cecil Ord)

Former London Midland & Scottish Railway (LMS) 2-6-2T No. 41251, shedded at Malton between 1959 and 1963, piloting ex-LNER Class B1 on the final pull into Goathland station from the north sometime in the late 1950s. The train is undoubtedly another returning seaside excursion. (Author's collection)

Swinging southwards through Newton Dale on 11 October 1961. (D. Hardy)

A deserted Whitby Town station in the mid-1950s, although there are trains at both number two and three platforms. On the extreme right, part of the stone-built York & North Midland Railway goods shed that was extensively damaged in the Second World War, with the much later brick signalbox attached to its corner. (J.W. Armstrong)

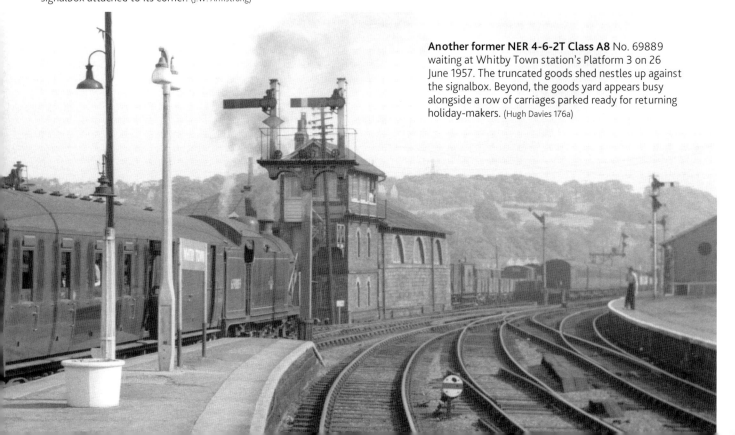

Another former NER 4-6-2T Class A8 No. 69889 waiting at Whitby Town station's Platform 3 on 26 June 1957. The truncated goods shed nestles up against the signalbox. Beyond, the goods yard appears busy alongside a row of carriages parked ready for returning holiday-makers. (Hugh Davies 176a)

The 6.57pm Whitby–Malton service battling up the 1 in 49 gradient between Grosmont and Goathland in the 1950s behind ex-NER 4-6-2T Class A8 No. 69861. The engine had been built at Darlington Works in 1913 and allocated to Whitby shed on two separate occasions in 1950 and 1952. It spent its last days at Malton until withdrawn in June 1960 after a creditable 46 years service. (Cecil Ord collection)

British Railways 2-6-0 Class 3 No. 77012 was an example of one of the smallest 'standard' class of locomotives designed for the nationalised railway. It was photographed at Darnholm hauling a Whitby–York train southwards on 5 September 1958, the cast 50G shed plate attached to its smokebox door indicating that at the time it was allocated to Whitby shed. (Cecil Ord collection)

But closures already agreed were not reversed, despite an ill-judged election campaign statement made by Harold Wilson MP that many took to mean the route through the North Yorkshire Moors would be protected. In the end, the only concession was that track and signalling were to be keep in situ between Grosmont and Goathland in case trains had to be used to carry school children in the winter. No track further south could be removed but other equipment could be recovered.

The last regular passenger trains between Whitby and Malton ran on Saturday 6 March 1965, with the addition of a steam special, 'The Whitby Moors', organised by the Stephenson Locomotive Society and the Manchester Locomotive Society, and run behind two preserved 2-6-0s, *The Great Marquess* and K1 No. 62005. Then as if to justify the retention of track, eight months after British Railways had withdrawn passenger trains on the line, it was called upon to run specials on 29 and 30 November 1965 as the school bus was unable to negotiate the snow between Whitby and Goathland. This gesture, however, was never repeated.

The need to move limestone away from the New Bridge quarry and bring in domestic coal to Pickering kept the line between there and Rillington Junction open for a further seven months until complete closure on 2 July 1966. By then, the Whitby to Pickering line had been in existence for almost exactly 130 years.

British Railways tickets. (P. Waller collection)

The signalman has just handed the Levisham–New Bridge (Pickering) single line token to the crew of Class B1 4-6-0 No. 61062 hauling this south-bound train entering Levisham station on 17 August 1963. It was just five months after publication of the 'Re-Shaping of British Railways' – the Beeching Report – proposing the closure of the whole route between Rillington Junction and Grosmont and the withdrawal of all passenger services to and from Whitby. Levisham station would be one of the casualties. (R.N. Joanes)

Pickering station as it looked at the end of its ownership by British Railways, the last timetabled passenger train running through on 6 March 1965. (D. Lawrence 5672a)

Revival

When the closure plans were announced, there were three good reasons put forward for retaining the line between Grosmont and Pickering. The first was to maintain a public service. The second was as a tourist attraction, a place where you could travel on a steam train. The third was as a way of controlling access to the North York Moors National Park (designated as such in 1952) by persuading visitors out of their cars and into trains. All three arguments were put forward immediately before and then after closure, but it was the second reason that initially triumphed over the others.

Two powerful drivers ensured the North Yorkshire Moors Railway (NYMR) emerged as a tourist attraction. The first was the timing of the closure. There had been widespread dismay at what the Beeching Plan of 1963 had wrought on the national rail network. In very few places had the case for closure of a line or station been successfully challenged. This impotency in the face of officialdom had inspired many to seek to run their own lines, spurred on by the achievement of the Bluebell Railway Preservation Society in 1960, and by the fighting spirit shown by other groups such as the one trying to reopen the Keighley & Worth Valley Railway.

These groups, and others that were emerging, were also symptoms of a wider reaction to the 1960s remodelling of the country's towns and cities and the replacement of Georgian and Victorian architecture with concrete tower blocks, shopping precincts and octopus-like road schemes. For a new generation, post-war modernisation had become tarnished. As the planners continued to pursue the demolish–rebuild happiness dream, there was an increasing number of ordinary people who were prepared to turn up at weekends and get their hands dirty digging out overgrown canals and rescuing all kinds of ordinary, 'working class' things that had been rapidly disappearing over the previous decade. These people were unpaid, it was not their job, they were not museum curators, but they wanted to preserve mills, mangles and milling machines, and perhaps the most emotive of all Victorian engineering achievements that were going to the scrap yards – steam locomotives.

The elimination of steam engines from British Railways in 1968 and the subsequent ban of running any but the *Flying Scotsman* on the national network after that date further encouraged the preservationists. If steam engines were to be seen, heard and smelt, then it had to be on private lines run by volunteers.

All this desire to preserve, however, would have borne different fruit if the NYMR had not passed through such inspiring scenery, and this was undoubtedly the second most important reason for the success of this railway as a tourist attraction. It is one of those ironies not always voiced, that although steam locomotives were products of an industrialised nation, in which the majority of the population lived and worked in towns and cities, most people go to visit them and travel behind them because they run in the countryside.

The First 25 Years (1967–1993)

British Railways had been obliged to leave the track *in situ* between Grosmont

Built in 1955, saddle tank 0-4-0 *Mirvale* was the first steam locomotive to be operated on the North Yorkshire Moors Railway (NYMR) by the new preservation society, at the beginning of 1969. The engine was named after the firm it originally worked for – Mirvale Chemicals in Mirfield. It is seen here at Goathland station on Easter Monday, 12 April 1971, only sixteen days after the North Yorkshire Moors Historical Railway Trust had been created. (Tony Wickens/Online Transport Archive/2604)

and Rillington Junction for two years after closure. As the expiry of this embargo approached, efforts to acquire the section of line between Grosmont and Pickering rested with the North Yorkshire Moors Railway Preservation Society (NYMRPS), formed in November 1967. With a price tag of £120,000 beyond the reach of the new group, the more realistic target became the purchase of all the trackbed, but only a single line of rails for 5.5 miles (8.85km) from Grosmont

Ticket No. 1051 issued by the NYMR at Goathland station on 27 June 1970 for two shillings (10p). (Author's collection)

Ticket No. 101, one of those issued on 27 June 1970 to members of the NYMR for travel between Grosmont and Ellerbeck, three years before the line was reopened through to Pickering. (Author's collection)

southwards through Goathland to the summit of the line near Ellerbeck (where the line came closest to the A169). The hope was to extend as future fundraising allowed. Membership of the society increased steadily, and by May 1969 it was able to pay British Railways a 10% deposit on the £42,500 asking price. If they had been unsure of the success of the society before, this event demonstrated to the North York Moors National Parks management that trains would soon be running into the heart of the Park and, rather than reduce the number of cars on local roads, it had the potential to encourage more.

Ellerbeck was remote enough, and the disruption caused by creating and then operating a new terminus for the railway there encouraged the Parks Committee and North Riding Council to offer to purchase for the NYMRPC a single track southwards from there to Pickering, thus creating an eighteen mile long preserved railway. In 1969, no preservation society anywhere in the country was operating more than a few miles of single track, but the society was prepared to rise to the challenge.

Grosmont became the centre of activities, with volunteers operating small tank steam locomotives at weekends and Bank Holidays to raise much needed funds. In June 1970 the North Eastern Locomotive Preservation Group's (NELPG) 1918-built NER Class T2 0-8-0, along with Lambton Tank 0-6-2T No. 29 built in 1904, were delivered to the railway. Two months later the latter's sister No. 5 arrived, to be joined in October the following year by the NELPG's 1923-built NER P3 Class 0-6-0. At the very end of that year, the North York Moors Historical Railway Trust (NYMHRT) was created to succeed the NYMRPS, becoming the first registered charity to operate a preserved railway. Paid staff were recruited to join the volunteers, the Light Railway Order for operating trains on the line was transferred from British Rail to the preservationists, and on 1 May 1973, the Duchess of Kent officially opened the North Yorkshire Moors Railway (NYMR). Steam trains for the paying public were then run between Grosmont and Goathland, with a diesel multiple unit (DMU) service to and from Levisham and the outskirts of Pickering.

The fact that trains were not able to use Pickering station at the time indicates that in the late 1960s and early 1970s not everyone was supportive of enthusiastic amateurs running railways.

Lined up in the down Platform 2 at Grosmont station on 20 May 1972 are *Mirvale* and Lambton Tank 0-6-2T, No. 29, the latter having been bought by NYMR and North Eastern Locomotive Preservation Group (NELPG) members in 1970. This engine was built in 1904 by Kitson & Co. of Leeds for working on the Lambton Colliery railway system. (Author's collection)

Brought to the NYMR in 1969, 0-6-0ST *Salmon* was built by Andrew Barclay & Sons of Kilmarnock in 1942 to work at Stewarts & Lloyds ironstone quarries in Lincolnshire. It was named after HMS Salmon, a British submarine sunk in 1940. Mirvale and Salmon were in steam at most open days, keeping the public interested and involved until a full passenger service could be operated. In this undated photograph, Salmon pulls an engineering train over the level crossing at Grosmont sometime between 1969 and 1971. (Author's collection)

In this photograph taken at Darnholm on 12 April 1971, Lambton Tank No. 5 is seen climbing the 1 in 49 towards Goathland only eight months after it had arrived on the NYMR. It was constructed by Robert Stephenson & Co. at Darlington in 1909 for use at Lambton Colliery, County Durham. Following a number of mergers with other collieries, by 1924 the Lambton Colliery had expanded its name to Lambton, Hetton & Joicey Collieries, explaining why 0-6-2T No. 5 and 0-6-2T No. 29 have been outshopped at various times in a livery with the initials of this post-1924 company. (Tony Wickens/Online Transport Archive /2609)

Only a month after the NYMR's service south of Goathland had begun, the diesel multiple unit (DMU) hired from British Rail stands at the temporary platform just north of Pickering on 28 May 1973. (Tony Wickens/Online Transport Archive /2604)

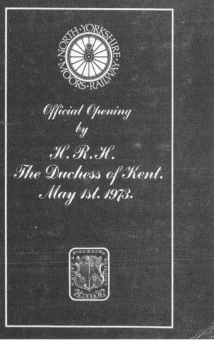

Front cover of the booklet issued to commemorate the opening of the NYMR by HRH The Duchess of Kent on 1 May 1973. (Author's collection)

Pottering about at Goathland in either the summer of 1972 or 1973, is 0-4-0ST No. 15 *Eustace Forth,* which had arrived on the railway in June 1972 and stayed until January 1978. It had been built in 1942 by Robert Stephenson and Hawthorns (a 1937 amalgamation of Robert Stephenson & Co. of Darlington and Hawthorn Leslie & Co. of Newcastle-upon-Tyne), and had been working before preservation at Dunston Power Station. (Stephenson Locomotive Society)

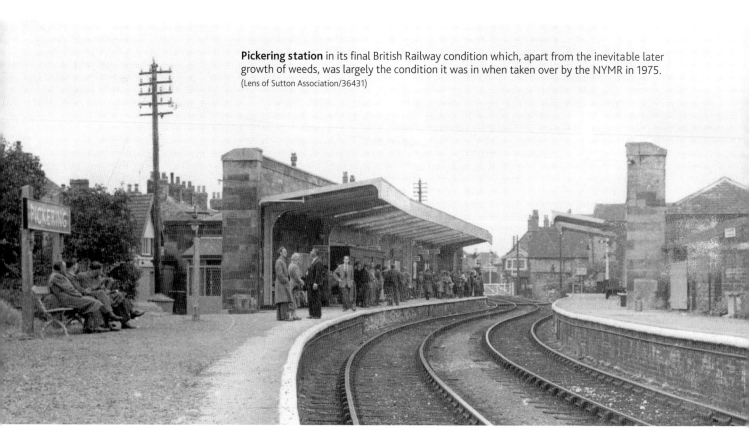

Pickering station in its final British Railway condition which, apart from the inevitable later growth of weeds, was largely the condition it was in when taken over by the NYMR in 1975. (Lens of Sutton Association/36431)

With the line through the town closed, Pickering Urban District Council had plans to modify the town's road layout by eliminating the level crossings on Bridge Street and Hungate and demolishing the station so that the site could be used for a supermarket and car park. The Council's application to compulsorily purchase the station site provoked a public enquiry at which Council representatives did not help their cause by describing the NYMR as '… a plaything for the affluent society.' A petition in favour of retaining the station was signed by 1,400 local residents with only 33 in opposition, and with over 75,000 tickets sold since passenger services restarted, the sensible outcome was that Pickering station should remain for the use of NYMR's trains.

Another Light Railway Order was granted and the station came back into use on 24 May 1975. With the public enquiry out of the way, Pickering Urban District Council wasted no time in demolishing the goods shed and coal drops between Bridge Street and Hungate, driving through a new road on the former track bed and laying out a public car park between those two roads.

For the new NYMR, the reverberations of the decision to operate the longest preserved railway in the country continued throughout that decade. The first chairman of the Trust, Richard Rowntree, expressed misgivings about the move away from a 'little' line that he believed could be run with volunteers, to one that might be considered as part of a strategy by others to keep road traffic out of a national park and would need far more resourcing than volunteers could muster. His opinion was supported, when in 1974 it was revealed that because British Rail were not able to provide second-hand track to repair and renew the line between Ellerbeck and Pickering at the £6,000 it had quoted, the NYMR had been obliged to spend in excess of

Former NER Class P3 0-6-0 No. 2392 inside the partly completed new locomotive shed south of Grosmont Tunnel in March 1973. After heading the NYMR re-opening train from Whitby on 1 May that year it went on to share the burden of hauling passenger services between Grosmont and Goathland with Lambton Tank No. 29, its partner in that re-opening train. The P3 was not worked as hard again until the early 1990s. (Author's collection)

£21,000 on renewals. The North York Moors National Park Committee was quickly made aware of this and agreed to inject £20,000 into track upgrading. In April 1981, when the single platform Newton Dale Halt was opened between Levisham and Goathland, it was primarily of benefit to those using the National Park rather than meeting any needs the NYMR might have had in that remote spot.

Throughout the 1970s, the NYMR attracted more and more volunteers, locomotives and rolling stock as passenger numbers also increased year on year. In 1977, some 250,000 passengers travelled on the line, and by the end of the 1981 season, that figure had risen to 320,000. (It is interesting to record that in that year, the annual wages bill of permanent staff employed by the railway amounted to £120,000, the same figure that British Rail had been asking for the purchase of the land and track between

Grosmont and Pickering back in 1967.) The NYMR had become the most popular heritage railway in the country.

But as with all emerging heritage railways, income from passengers never covered operating costs, and so bank loans kept the trains running in those early years. Capital expenditure was also severely restricted by what could be raised from special appeals, and whereas other preserved lines constituted as limited companies, or with such supporting organisations, began to raise capital by share issues during this period, the NYMR was constrained by being a registered charity with no trading arm. In 1984/5, the Trust looked on enviously at the Severn Valley Railway (SVR) as it extended to Kidderminster and

Former NER Class T2 0-8-0 No. 2238 with a full head of steam outside 'Tunnel Cottages', Grosmont on 9 October 1976. The whole scene gives a good impression of the early years of the NYMR when enthusiasm and hard physical work were the main ingredients for keeping the trains running. Until 1989 the cottages provided accommodation for volunteers. (Author's collection)

raised funds at such a rate that it was immediately able to construct a new, large brick terminal station based on authentic Great Western Railway architecture, and have enough left over to finance the building of a brand new sixty-seven lever signalbox with all the associated signalling (completed in 1987).

In 1986, the first ideas for a lavish revamp of Whitby station that would rival the Kidderminster creation were aired in 'Moors Line' (No. 74) – the magazine of the North York Moors Historical Railway Trust. This started the discussions as to whether the NYMR would ever be able to fund such a project if it could not resort to issuing shares. With the

inevitable answer being no, it was no surprise that at the last Council meeting of 1987, the Chairman of the NYMHRT proposed a share issue. This in turn led to a study into the benefits or otherwise of setting up a plc, the interim report being submitted at the end of 1989. Official blessing to such a move was ratified by the NYMHRT on 7 July 1990, leading to the immediate formation of the North Yorkshire Moors Railway Enterprise plc (NYMRE plc).

The first meeting of the new organisation was held twelve days later and then on 8 August a share issue was launched at Grosmont with the National Railway Museum's replica *Rocket* in attendance. The aim was to raise £500,000 for a portfolio of projects ranging from improving the motive power depot (MPD) at Grosmont to extending the platforms at Pickering. By October

£150,000 had been subscribed and when the issue was closed at the end of 1991, the total stood at £245,000.

Unfortunately, that success was soon overshadowed by dissent amongst the 'rank and file' of the railway, concerned about increased commercialism and conflicting priorities. A few unpleasant years followed in which disputes made headlines outside the railway, consultants were brought in, there were resignations and the roles of the new plc and the existing NYMHRT were reappraised.

What helped restore a balance in the railway's affairs were the challenges brought about by a national recession, and the phenomenal popularity of a new Independent Television (ITV) series – 'Heartbeat'. Passenger numbers were quickly restored to those of the 1980s boom years and most people associated with the NYMR found they had a common purpose once again.

Of crucial importance to the survival of the NYMR for the next twenty-five years, as with all heritage railways, was compromise. There have been, and will probably continue to be, tensions between preservation and commercialism, and preservation and operation. The aims and priorities of one group of railway enthusiasts will be different to those of another and there will also be tensions in relation to how operations are carried out and provided for the paying customer. The passage of time also effects how decisions are viewed and the following selective examples will illustrate some of those tensions.

Motive Power

For most of its existence, the NYMR has operated but not owned locomotives. From the beginning, owners of engines were attracted to the line because their machines could be worked hard over a long challenging section of line including a gradient of 1 in 49. To manage their use, the NYMR set up

two forms of locomotive agreement: a service agreement whereby the NYMR maintained, repaired and overhauled the engines using its own staff and resources; and a mileage or historic locomotive agreement in which the owners undertook their own maintenance, repair etc using their own volunteers. Since 1969 those two agreements have been revised on a number of occasions when either the NYMR or the locomotive owners have felt they were not getting value for money. When the line opened in 1973, steam

Sporting its former British Railways livery and number, 0-8-0 Class Q6 No. 63395 pulls away purposely from Grosmont on 3 April 2016 with a special birthday party train. The engine was built at Darlington in 1918 by the NER as No. 2238, a member of the large class of T2 locomotives. It was purchased by NELPG in 1968, restored, and ran its first trains on the NYMR in 1970. When this photograph was taken, it had been in preservation for 48 years (1968–2016) only one year less than the time it had spent working, firstly for the NER, then the LNER and finally British Railways (1918–1967). (Author)

Ex-LNER Class A4 No. 60007 *Sir Nigel Gresley* approaching Goathland Summit on 6 October 2013 with a south-bound train. The locomotive was built at Doncaster in 1937 and named after its illustrious designer. With the end of steam traction on British Railways rapidly approaching, a group was set up in 1964 specifically to preserve the engine once it was declared redundant. This happened in 1966 and the locomotive passed into the care of the A4 Preservation Society. The locomotive first came to the NYMR in 1999, after which it became an important visitor attraction for the railway. (Author)

Shortly after another major overhaul, Lambton Tank No. 29 waits to depart from Goathland station on 12 May 2013 with an ex-Great Northern Railway saloon built in 1909. Of all the industrial locomotives that worked on the NYMR during the 1970s it was only this engine and No. 5 that stayed, continuing to perform into the twenty-first century, working alongside more powerful main line locomotives, both resident on the line and visiting from other heritage railways. (Author)

A view from above the tunnels at Grosmont in April 1973. Class P3 0-6-0 No. 2392 stands on the Y&NMR bridge over the River Musk Esk. It was the operation of this engine, alongside former NER 0-8-0 Class T2 No. 2238 (63395), the two Lambton Tanks and LMS 'Black Five' 4-6-0 No. 45428 from 1974, that very quickly propelled the NYMR into the premier league of heritage railways. (Author's collection)

British Railways Class 24 No. D5032, built in 1959 and saved from the scrap yard in 1976 for use on the NYMR. Photographed leaving Grosmont Tunnel on 11 April 2010. (Author)

this title reinforced the view of the then chairman that this section of line was really being operated, unofficially, on behalf of the North York Moors National Park Committee. When it was suggested steam locomotives should replace the DMUs, controversy was stirred by the assertion they would have to be altered to burn oil instead of coal to eliminate the danger of sparks setting fires in Newton Dale. The conversions never took place, and in 1976 the NYMR proudly announced it was to run coal-fired, steam locomotives working over the whole route between Grosmont and Pickering every Sunday from 11 July for eight Sundays, plus Bank Holiday Mondays (19 April and 30 August), with the addition of eight special charter trains. Unfortunately, that summer turned out to be one of the driest on record, and services through the National Park had to be hauled by the increasing number of main line diesels taking up residence at Grosmont.

The most iconic of those diesels were two British Railways Class 55 engines – *Alycidon* and *Royal Highland Fusilier*, members of a fleet of twenty-two locomotives used to operate the principal services over the East Coast main line between 1961 and 1981. In August 1982, the Deltic Preservation Society (DPS) chose to set up its base at the railway with these two machines. Their use, with the other diesels, to haul passenger trains, however, divided opinion amongst both enthusiasts and visitors. In 1985, DMU services on the line ended, and in 1986 more trains were timetabled for steam haulage, 'Moors Line' (No. 86) reporting that the first train out of Pickering was poorly patronised because it was diesel hauled, passengers preferring to wait to ride on a steam train.

In May 1987 *Royal Highland Fusilier* left for the Midland Railway Trust in Derbyshire because the NYMR had been unable to provide undercover accommodation promised to the DPS at

locomotives were used only to haul trains between Grosmont and Goathland. Between there and Pickering, DMUs were purchased by the NYMR to operate a shuttle service. In that year, these were out-shopped in a new corporate livery of green and cream with a painted headboard reading 'The National Park Scenic Cruise'. Perhaps unintentionally,

British Rail Class 55 'Deltic' No. D9009 *Alycidon,* photographed on 6 May 2007 pulling alongside Platform 2 at Grosmont, with Platform 1, part of the national rail network used by trains between Whitby and Middlesbrough, on the right. The Deltic was one of twenty-two that worked the principal expresses along the East Coast main line between 1961 and 1981. It was named after the 1949 Ascot Gold Cup winning horse, and after withdrawal in January 1982 was purchased by the Deltic Preservation Society. (Author)

New Bridge for storage and maintenance. For the 1989 season, the NYMR introduced an almost all-steam timetable with only occasional 'diesel days', following that up in 1990 by confining diesel working to Saturdays only in July and August. That same year, *Alycidon* moved away, although it did return for brief stays in 1998, 2007, 2008 and 2013. By 1992, the editor of 'Moors Line' (No. 95) was able to confidently write: '…Track to run on, rolling stock to ride in and stations to commence and finish journeys are essential, but first and foremost it is the steam locomotive that visitors come to see.'

Nevertheless, the running of diesels and the holding of dedicated 'diesel galas' continued (and still does at the time of writing), and for younger generations who have never witnessed diesels at work on the national network, they have become as historically interesting as the steam engines they replaced.

Creating facilities for the restoration, repair and maintenance of locomotives has also involved NYMR management in some difficult decision making over the years. The area immediately south of Grosmont Tunnel was initially the only space where locomotives could be serviced and since then a fully equipped Motive Power Depot (MPD) and other restoration workshops have been

The 1973 Grosmont shed with its recently completed brick façade. Standing next to 'Tunnel Cottages' is John Fowler & Co. of Leeds 0-4-0 diesel-mechanical shunter No. 21, built in 1955 and converted into a diesel hydraulic in 1966, one of the many small industrial locomotives that were brought to the railway by various individuals and groups of enthusiasts in the 1970s. This particular one had worked for British Steel, Hartlepool, before remaining on the NYMR for twenty-seven years. (Author's collection)

Another powerful former NER locomotive to have worked on the NYMR is 0-8-0 Class T3 No. 901, seen here at Grosmont on 27 April 1991. The engine was built to a Sir Vincent Raven design in 1919, and was reclassified Class Q7 in LNER ownership. It worked from various sheds, was taken into British Railway stock in 1948, and not withdrawn until December 1962. It was preserved as part of the National Collection and in 1979 the NELPG began a major overhaul at Grosmont. In the year this photograph was taken, it achieved a mileage of 2,898 miles on the NYMR. (Author's collection)

Running into Pickering station in July 2002 is former Southern Railway 'Schools' Class 4-4-0 No. 30926 *Repton,* built in 1934. After withdrawal in 1962 it went to the Steamtown railway museum, USA, in 1966, before repatriation in 1989 and restoration at Grosmont. When this locomotive came to the NYMR it prompted a review of the track and bridges on the line as the engine had a heavier axle load than engines used up until then. (Author's collection)

LNER 0-8-0 Class Q6 No. 63395 again, this time making steady progress on the 1 in 49 climb through Darnholm on the approach to Goathland station, Sunday 15 May 2016. Behind the engine are six beautifully restored teak carriages, their colour complementing the lush spring greenery and the flowering gorse bushes. (Author)

Deviation signalbox,
Grosmont,
photographed on
12 October 1968. It
had closed as a block
post in 1930 but was
retained as a ground
frame under the control
of ('released from')
Grosmont signalbox
and only used when
access was needed to
the Beck Hole branch
line. (Tony Wickens/Online
Transport Archive /2438)

developed there. The first steel-framed
shed was erected between 1972 and 1973.
Back then, the only buildings on the site
were Deviation signalbox and a terrace
of Victorian brick cottages that became
volunteer accommodation. (The signalbox
was the oldest on the line, dating from the
forming of a junction between the original
course of the Whitby & Pickering Railway
and the new line through to Goathland
Mill, opened in 1865.)

Despite this, as the need grew to
provide more undercover accommodation
for the storage, maintenance and overhaul
of locomotives, the decision was made
to demolish the signalbox in 1977 to
make way for another locomotive shed
('Deviation Shed'). Four years earlier, in
the Spring 1973 edition of 'Moors Line'
(No. 23), the Civil Engineer had written
in relation to the possible demolition: 'Do
we preserve the box which is of no direct
use to the railway or provide essential
facilities for the historic steam engines on

the only site available?' Expressed here
is the dilemma of railway preservation:
preservation for its own sake, or
preservation for use?

Deviation Shed, which came from
the Longmoor Military Training Camp,
was financed and built by the NELPG,
the frame erected in May 1978 and the
roof and cladding added during the
summer. By 1982, there were twenty-
nine locomotives on the Grosmont site
in various states from working order to a
kit of parts. The pressure to improve the
facilities during that decade continued to
be irresistible and by the start of the 1990s
the site had been transformed into what
looked something like a small MPD at the
end of steam on British Railways.

In 1988, using Manpower Services
Commission (MSC) labour, a new brick
mess/amenity block was built on the
north end of the 1973 shed. This block
was officially opened on 29 October
that year. By then the decision had been

Former NER 0-8-0 No. 63395 once again, this time resting alongside visiting ex-Somerset & Dorset 2-8-0 No. 53809 in Grosmont running shed on 3 April 2011. (Author)

made that the row of Victorian cottages that were still being used by volunteers had to go. In early 1989, the southern section was demolished, then at the end of July that year the last three occupants left, and between then and Christmas, the remainder of the row was cleared away so that the area could be used to store locomotive boilers. In October 1989, the only mechanical coaling tower on a heritage railway was brought into use close by, and in the New Year, a new running shed was constructed immediately to the east and adjoining the 1973 shed. In 1991, Deviation Shed was reclad and provided with better public access and was formally opened on 16 June of that year by NELPG President, Bill Harvey.

This rapid redevelopment of Grosmont MPD, lead to even more ambitious plans. In the summer 1989 edition of 'Moors Line' (No. 84) proposals were unveiled for the creation of a complex of workshops, museum displays and picnic areas on land to the south-east of the site that had been purchased in 1987. The complex was to be named the 'John Bellwood Museum' after the NYMR's one time General Manager and subsequent Chief Mechanical Engineer of the National Railway Museum, who had died in 1988. After the creation of the NYME plc in 1990 it was proposed to use some of the moneys raised through the share issue to finance this project, and although a start was made in July 1991 when the site was levelled by the Territorial Army, 'The John Bellwood Centre' as it had been rechristened progressed no further.

In 1997 a new fabrication shop partly funded by a European grant was erected in front of the 1973 shed, and then a few years later a brick structure was erected on the west side of the running lines to house Armstrong Oilers, a 1907 firm taken over by the NYMR in 2005.

British Railways Class 9F 2-10-0 No. 92214 under the coaling tower outside Deviation Shed, Grosmont on 15 April 2012. Following an overhaul the previous year it was named *Cock o' the North,* but did not stay on the NYMR for long, being purchased by a Great Central Railway plc director in 2014 and quickly moved to Loughborough. (Author)

The coaling tower next to Deviation Shed was brought into use in October 1989 as part of a major redevelopment of the area immediately south of Grosmont tunnel that had been first used at the end of the 1960s to prepare steam locomotives for their daily work. (Author)

Carriages

The story of carriage repair and restoration on the NYMR has also had its ups and downs. In the 1970s there was pressure to paint all the operational passenger carriages in a 'corporate livery' unique to the NYMR. To the relief of many railway enthusiasts, this did not happen, and since then vehicles have appeared in the liveries most appropriate to their original railway owners and their age. One of the best results of this policy has been the creation of a set ('rake') of beautifully restored LNER teak carriages.

The carcases of a number of these distinctive LNER vehicles had been some of the earliest arrivals to the NYMR, but the real impetus towards their restoration to original condition came in 1979. In that year the last remaining examples still owned by British Rail were put up for sale by tender. When the Council of the NYMHRT could not be persuaded to put in a bid, a group of members of the Trust got together to form the LNER Coaching Association (LNERCA), one of their number immediately purchasing the group's first vehicle. They based themselves at Pickering to begin the laborious task of restoration. The group aimed for the highest standards of restoration, seeking out not just the correct replacement timber but also period fittings. Nothing upset them more than an innocent remark in the winter 1983/84 edition of 'Moors Line' (No. 66) that as there was an urgent need for more carriages LNER examples should be put back into revenue-earning service regardless of authentic fittings and livery!

At first the LNERCA was able to source a log of teak that was sawn to the lengths required for replacement panelling of a limited size. Then sheets of teak were imported from Bangkok and Singapore, allowing a number of LNER carriages to be restored not only at Pickering but also by other preservation

Behind Baldwin 2-8-0 No. 6046, five former LNER teak carriages all carefully restored at Pickering, form a train reminiscent of travel during the Second World War. The range from white to dark grey of the carriage roofs gives an indication of how long each vehicle had been in service. (Author)

societies at other railway heritage sites around the country. But the most interesting source of good timber was purchased in the late 1990s. This was a teak log, 40ft (12.2m) long with a cross-section tapering from 3ft (1m) to 2ft (0.6m) that had been recovered along with over 20 others from the wreck of the steamship *Pegu*, sunk on 8 July 1917 when it hit a British-laid mine during its voyage from Rangoon to Liverpool and Glasgow. Most of the logs were acquired for work on HMS *Victory*, but given that there was no chance of finding a similar log that could be cut into both the lengths and widths required to replace

complete panels on LNER carriages, the LNERCA felt the asking price of £25,000 was a wise investment. The association's first LNER carriage was put back into traffic, fully restored, in 1994 (Gresley buffet No. 641) and ten years later members were looking after twenty-four wooden carriages dating from the 1890s to 1950, including seven LNER carriages running on the NYMR.

The restoration of other carriages by the NYMR's own small Carriage & Wagon team has not required the sourcing of material from such unusual locations, but it has involved them in an equivalent amount of painstaking work. For both groups, the task was eased in the 1980s by the erection of a 100ft (30m) long by 40ft (12m) wide two road shed and, ironically, the reinstatement of a

In 1979 the LNER Coach Association was inaugurated, basing its operations at Pickering. Since then, volunteers working for the Association have restored a number of teak coaches, this 1930 brake third No. 3669 nearing completion when photographed at Pickering on 4 October 2013. It was officially 'unveiled' in May 2015 by Tim Godfrey, the grandson of its designer, Sir Nigel Gresley. (Author)

With locomotive and carriages all in authentic historic liveries, this 2013 view at Moorgates, just south of Goathland station, replicates perfectly a scene from the mid-1950s. Locomotive and carriages are a testament to the hard work of many volunteers over many years. (Author)

turntable at Pickering. Work started on the new building in the summer of 1983, and between then and 1996, a complex of buildings was created, funded from a number of sources, including Yorkshire & Humberside Museums & Art Gallery Service. The turntable project involved the excavation and enlargement of the existing pit and then the installation of the 60ft (18.3m) table from the National Railway Museum, rendered redundant in 1991 when 'The Great Hall' at York was being refurbished. (Many years before, the NYMR had salvaged a 55ft (16.8m) turntable from Neville Hill, Leeds, but had not been able to re-use it.) The work at Pickering was completed for the 1993 season.

No heritage railway can consistently run trains that replicate a specific historic period, but occasionally the date and liveries of the locomotive and the carriage behind do match, and this was just such a time at Grosmont on 11 May 2012. Visiting A4 No. 4464 *Bittern* in its 1937 livery was coupled to a train of five former LNER carriages restored to their original teak condition. (Author)

The most recent shed – The Atkins Building – was completed in 2008 and opened at the end of September that year by Pete Waterman. The public can access this building from the carpark and not only see progress on carriage restoration but also talk to the volunteers. Turning out and maintaining carriages in the most efficient way remains vital to the success of the NYMR, especially as all visitors travelling on the line will spend much of their time in these vehicles, which will leave them with a lasting impression of the railway.

Perhaps the ultimate travelling experience in NYMR carriages has been the Pullman services. By the 1980s authentic Pullman cars and modified and reliveried British Railways Mark One carriages had been brought together to form a 'Pullman' train. Although the fundamental concept of the premium service this train was able to provide has remained the same, the way it has been marketed and delivered has changed over the years. In the early 1980s the 'North Yorkshire Pullman' became very popular as an evening dining experience every Wednesday between May and September, running out and back between Pickering and Goathland. For the 1985 season the catering was contracted out and more carriages were added to the train so that more customers could be accommodated. A Thursday evening departure was added to the timetable and all services were extended so as to run the entire length of the line from Pickering to Grosmont. After further refurbishment of vehicles, other services were offered including a Sunday lunchtime train, 'The Moorlander', a Friday evening 'The Pickering Pullman', and a festive 'The Christmas Moorlander'.

At the time of writing, daytime services are marketed as the 'Kingthorpe Pullman', 'Moorlander Sunday Lunch' or 'Pullman Afternoon Tea', with evening

During the 2013 'LNER Gala Weekend', visiting twenty-first century A1 4-6-2 *Tornado* confidently climbs the 1 in 49 gradient at Water Ark on 6 October with the Pullman Dining Train. (Author)

The 10.30am departure from Grosmont behind A4 *Sir Nigel Gresley*, 5 October 2013. (Author)

trains advertised as the 'Pickering Pullman', 'North Yorkshire Pullman' and the 'Battersby Pullman Dining'. There are also special seasonal services and other occasional specials utilising the Pullman train, but what ever the manifestation and nomenclature, and in whatever form, it remains popular and is an important source of income for the NYME plc.

Stations

The standard of all NYMR stations also affects the visitor experience and here there is always tension between preservation and the provision of facilities demanded by twenty-first century families. During the 1980s the NYMR struggled with the basics such as toilets, ticket sales, shops and refreshments. The several, small, plywood kiosks erected on the platform at Pickering in the late 1970s to cope with some of these requirements were not popular but their use was defended in

the Autumn 1981 'Moors Line' (No. 57) article as 'regrettable but necessary'. Five years later they were removed along with the two BR Mark I coaches that had been parked at the south end of Platform 1 to provide refreshments.

As recorded elsewhere, passenger numbers continued to increase throughout the 1980s, not only putting pressure on station facilities but also in the way trains could be handled at platforms. The short, branch line platforms inherited by the NYMR could not cope with the length of trains and the volume of people using them. Extending the platforms was the sensible operational solution, but it had to be balanced against the dilution of the historic atmosphere of the stations. The public were drawn to the NYMR to savour that atmosphere and not just to get on and off trains as quickly and safely as possible. In 1988, plans for a major upgrade of the visitor facilities at Goathland station included suggestions to

An unusually quiet Goathland station photographed at the beginning of a new operating season in April 2013. The footbridge made up of standard cast-iron parts, is a good example of what became a familiar feature at many NER stations. This one, however, was not installed at Goathland until 1985, but it looks as though it has always been there. (Author)

During the Scottish Branch Line Gala weekend in May 2016, 'Black Five' 4-6-0 No. 45428 was given the number of another member of the same class – No. 45066 – and the shed plate 66A, to commemorate that locomotive's last years at Polmadie MPD, Glasgow. It was photographed on 14 May 2016 from a very popular photographic spot just south of Goathland station, pulling away with the 4.24pm to Pickering. (Author)

extend the down platform, which would have required the original NER signalbox to be rebuilt elsewhere. Fortunately, this was considered too great an alteration, and one no doubt management was pleased they had not backed when the visual appeal of the existing station was one of the deciding factors in ITV choosing to film many 'Heartbeat' scenes at the station.

Nevertheless, platform extensions were considered necessary at Grosmont and Pickering no matter the historic and visual impact. In 1989, BR completed the re-alignment of the Esk Valley line at the former so that the NYMR could extend Platform 2 northwards to accommodate ten-coach trains. The work was completed in stages, benefitting from the recovery of 115 stone platform coping stones from

the redundant Helmsley station in March 1990 so that the job could be completed for the end of the year. Between May and August the following year, Platform 1 at Pickering was extended by contractors, and during 2003 Platforms 3 and 4 at Grosmont were extended.

As well as these changes, at Goathland and Pickering the NYMR also erected footbridges between platforms to reduce the use of the barrow crossings at these places that had always been a potential danger for both passengers and staff crossing the lines. Both these bridges were authentic NER cast-iron examples, the one

At the north end of Grosmont station a Northern Railways' train comes in from Whitby whilst on the right, the NYMR's train waits at Platform 2 for its timetabled slot with the 11.10am departure for the seaside town, 3 April 2016. The Esk Valley line here was realigned to allow the NYMR's down platform to be extended in 1990. (Author)

re-erected at Goathland in 1985/6 with financial assistance from Scarborough District Council coming from Howden station. The same pattern of footbridge for Pickering was acquired from Walker Gate, Tyneside, and was originally part of a plan to link the catering coaches parked next to an extended up platform to the down platform so that the barrow crossing could be eliminated at the south

end of the station. Just over £2,500 was raised for this work, but the catering plan, along with the southern extension of the platform, was abandoned and, with the bridge project put on hold, the money went towards the Goathland bridge. The barrow crossing was eventually replaced by a new path around the buffer stops but a bridge between platforms north of the main station building was still useful as it would shorten the distance visitors had to walk from the car park (opened in 1981) at the west of the carriage works to the booking office on platform one. The bridge was brought into use in April 1997.

A number of authentic NER timber buildings have also been rebuilt at NYMR stations, successfully enhancing their environment. For example, at Pickering buildings from Gilling and Whitby have been re-erected, at Goathland a workshop was created from a warehouse from Whitedale station and at Grosmont, the booking office on Platform 2 came from Sleights. What completely transformed the whole environment of Pickering station for the better, however, was the installation of an overall roof to replicate the Y&NMR one that had been removed by British Railways in 1952. The work was part of a larger project to refurbish all the surviving structures there. An appeal was launched in 1995 and a Heritage Lottery Fund (HLF) award of £330,000 was secured in 1998. With matching funds, this enabled the main stone buildings to be re-roofed, internal floors brought up to platform level, the booking office improved and other cosmetic upgrades achieved for the 2000 season. The final phase, which included the creation of a new learning centre and the fabrication and fitting of the overall roof, became possible following the award of an HLF grant of almost £1m, combined with support from the Regional Development Agency for Yorkshire and the Humber

The brand new overall roof at Pickering, receiving the final finishing touches in April 2011. (Author)

The authentic detailing of the braced trusses supporting the 2011 timber and slate roof at Pickering is a credit to the designers, as they had obviously taken much care in replicating those used for G.T. Andrews' original roofs at various stations on the Y&NMR. Unfortunately, since this photograph was taken, soot deposited from steam locomotives has obscured the subtle colouring of the individual components. (Author)

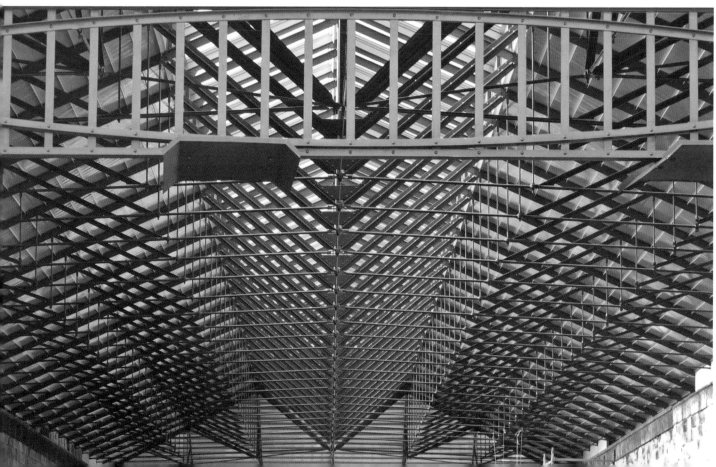

Externally the new 2010–11 roof at Pickering was not an exact replica of the original 1845 one. The profile of the eaves was to the more generous proportions adopted by G.T. Andrews at Filey station where the roof had been restored in 2009. Photograph taken in April 2016. (Author)

in September 2008. Sufficient matching public donations were forthcoming for work to take place through the winter of 2010/11, and fittingly, considering the outstanding quality of design and workmanship, the whole project gained the top award in the 2012 National Railway Heritage Awards sponsored by Ian Allan Publishing.

Civil Engineering and Permanent Way

In these areas of the NYMR's responsibilities, it is perhaps only signalling that is ever noticed by visitors. The majority will never see the bridges their train crosses during their journeys or the track on which it runs. But the maintenance and periodic renewal of these components of the railway is vital to the running of a safe service and it is in

these areas that the biggest 'preservation' compromises have had to be made.

In 1973, the NYMR took over a line that was run down. There were thirty-seven bridges (including viaducts) and two tunnels, the masonry overbridges needing little attention but all the bridges made up either entirely of wrought-iron or of iron and timber in need of repair work. The single track (permanent way) that was inherited was mostly formed of 45ft (13.7m) and some 60ft (18.3m) lengths of bull head rail, supported in cast chairs, bolted to timber sleepers set in ash or very light ballast. On the tightest curves – and there were many – there was an additional line of rails called a 'check rail', positioned to help prevent wheel flanges of locomotives and rolling stock from riding up over the rail tops. At all the stations the layouts had been compromised by

British Railways 2-6-0 Class 4MT No. 76079 storming into Goathland station with a train from Whitby on 2 April 2016. It is running over traditional track made up of bullhead rail supported in cast chairs bolted to timber sleepers, the turnout in the foreground being laid by volunteers in the first years of the heritage line's history. The lower quadrant NER signal was also an NYMR addition, as was the earth bank at the end of the truncated former down line provided to stop any vehicle rolling out of the station and down the 1 in 49 grade. (Author)

the removal of the second running line, and at Pickering, British Rail had made rushed rationalisations in between the cessation of passenger services and the end of coal traffic between there and Rillington Junction.

The tasks before the NYMR's new Civil Engineering Department were daunting, but the work was approached in a professional manner despite the limitations of volunteer labour. The priority was to make the NYMR infrastructure fit for purpose; preservation was a secondary consideration. Where

old equipment could not be repaired, it would be replaced with new because that was the way things were done on a professional railway.

During the winter of 1973, work started on altering the track layout at New Bridge, Pickering, and on installing a turnout at the north end of Levisham station to create a loop. The work was hard, relying on muscle power and camaraderie. Two years later, the crossovers at the summit of the line just south of Goathland, which had been used by engines running round their trains in the very early years of the NYMR, were removed. In the same year the first repairs were made to what was thought at the time to be steel decking plates in bridge No. 30 (see later). By 1977 the new track layout at Pickering was complete and had involved a lot of rearrangement, including the slewing of the track over High Mill crossing (up side to down side) and the taking out of the former down line at New Bridge level crossing and then slewing the track north of there to rejoin the remaining down track. In 1978, bridge No.10 near Farworth was the first to be fitted with a new concrete deck to replace the corroded metal one. Bridges 14 and 15 were similarly treated later in the 1980s. During February and March 1982, the track, ballast and infill of the arches of Esk Valley Viaduct (bridge No. 37) south of Grosmont, was removed so that a new waterproof membrane could be installed. In another major civil engineering exercise carried out between November 1987 and January 1988, bridges number 16 and 17, about three miles north of Levisham at Gallock Hill, were eliminated altogether by diverting Pickering Beck into a new channel. These are just a few examples of the achievements in just two decades of the NYMR's history, but the jobs were – and always will be – never ending.

By the end of the 1980s, the Civil Engineering Department had managed to develop a dedicated depot in a field owned by the NYMR at New Bridge for the equipment it had acquired since the 1970s (including track vehicles and a steam crane) and for the deliveries of rail, sleepers, etc. Work had started on this in the summer of 1982 when two sidings were run in off the main line. In 1987, planning permission was sought for a two road shed, which was initially refused by the North York Moors National Park Planning Committee. When the application was passed the following year, fund-raising began, but it was not until 1993 that work started on laying the foundations and erecting the frame of the shed. In the next few years, however, the site was extended and became to the Civil Engineering

Department what Grosmont MPD had become for the locomotive engineers, assuming all the qualities of a British Rail or Network Rail depot.

If proof was needed that civil engineering did indeed underpin the railway's operation, it came in the winter of 2009/10 when bridge No. 30 at Water Ark was replaced. The 1865 bridge over the Eller Beck at this remote location comprised a double-track, riveted, wrought-iron deck supported on stone piers either side of the river, which was crossed on the skew. It was the largest single metal span bridge inherited by the NYMR, and had been strengthened on a number of occasions and been carefully monitored since the 1970s. With the aim of maintaining the whole route for an axle load of twenty-two tons so as to allow the use of the largest main line steam locomotives, the ability of bridge No. 30 to cope with those loads had to be tackled. The decision was made to replace it with an uncompromising single track structure made up of steel beams supporting a concrete deck. The priority was to maintain the operation of the railway in the most efficient and practical way possible.

A £1m appeal was launched to raise the necessary money (which would also go towards the restoration of BR 2-6-4T Class 4MT No. 80135), attracting much high-profile endorsement and media coverage. As with all track renewals, the work had to be carried out during the closed season when revenue-earning trains were not running, and by 2009, that had narrowed down to a January. Contractors were employed to both dismantle the old bridge and erect the replacement, and their task was made almost impossibly difficult by heavy snowfall and freezing conditions. Despite this, removal was completed by the end of January and the new bridge was ready for the first passenger train of the 2010 season, which crossed southbound

Former LMS 'Black Five' No. 45428 crossing bridge No. 30 at Water Ark on 2 April 2016. The single track steel span bridge with cast concrete deck replaced the 1860s wrought-iron double track structure in the winter of 2010. As described in the main text, it was a challenging operation, not apparent from this view dominated by a hard-working locomotive. (Author)

on 27 March. As one of the prominent supporters of the project, Pete Waterman carried out the official opening ceremony on 19 April 2010.

The track relaid across bridge No. 30 was flat-bottom rail on concrete sleepers, a pattern and specification that had become the standard on the NYMR and on the national rail network. Concrete sleepers had become the preferred

replacement to traditional timber ones right at the start of the NYMR's involvement with the line.

Back in 1979 the Civil Engineer had reported in the Autumn edition of 'Moors Line' (No. 49) that his aim was to replace 4,000 timber sleepers each year for five or six years with concrete replacements. In reporting that flat bottom rail would be installed at Fen Bog, he went on to say: 'Flat bottom rail will last longer than bull head rail and hence in future, when we need to change the rail at the same time as the sleepers, we will endeavour to use this type of rail.'

By the end of the first decade of the twenty-first century, there was very little traditional bull head rail left in use on the running lines. Most of the check rails had been removed and ash had been superseded everywhere by stone ballast. There was much satisfaction felt by the civil engineering and permanent way teams in this achievement as there was in the next two logical advances made over the winter of 2014/15. At Beck Hole, as well as relaying with flat bottom rail on concrete sleepers, a three quarter mile long stretch was laid on steel sleepers with the rail welded up to form

A restored rake of former British Railways Mark 1 carriages, in matching late 1950s maroon livery, being hauled up the gradient at Water Ark by ex-LNER Class B1 on 6 October 2013. The train has just passed over a section of bullhead track on concrete sleepers that replaced the track inherited by the NYMR at this location, and is running onto a recently laid section of flat-bottom track carried on concrete sleepers. As elsewhere on the line, during relaying, stone ballast replaced the ash that once supported the sleepers. The track alignment was also altered slightly to take advantage of the double track formation. (Author)

continuous runs over that section. This latest innovation has not been without its critics, but the logic is undeniable: flat-bottom rail and matching track components can be acquired new, and eliminating rail joints every 60ft (18.3m) as with standard track, requires less maintenance, an important consideration

Visiting the NYMR in 2009, new-build 4-6-2 Class A1 No. 60163 approaches
Levisham. Unlike at New Bridge, Pickering, the signalbox here survived with its lever
frame intact and was subsequently re-locked to control the changed track layout
developed by the NYMR's emerging S&T (Signal & Telegraph) Department in the
1970s. (Author)

on any heritage railway with limited
human resources and particularly on
one eighteen miles in length. How long
traditional bullhead rail supported in cast
chairs can or should be retained at NYMR
stations is open to question.

Signalling

Although the signalboxes at Goathland
Summit and those either end of Pickering
station at High Mill and Bridge Street
remained when British Railways
closed the line, they did not survive
into preservation. What did pass into
NYMR ownership were the signalboxes
at Grosmont, Deviation Junction,
Goathland, Newton Dale, Levisham, and
New Bridge (just north of Pickering). The
fate of Deviation signalbox has already
been chronicled.

The first signalbox to be brought
back into use was that at Levisham,
recommissioned on 10 May 1975
when the passing loop there had been
completed. A number of original NER
lower quadrant signals that had been
brought in from elsewhere were made
operational between then and the end
of the summer season. With the opening
of Levisham box, 'One Engine in Steam'
working was introduced between there
and Pickering. The following year,
controversy was caused when lifting
barriers with accompanying flashing
warning road signals were brought

As part of the Scottish Branch Line Gala for Sunday 15 May 2016, 'Black Five' No. 45428 was temporarily numbered No. 45049 and fitted with the shed plate 63B for Stirling, where that particular engine had been shedded between September 1956 and August 1963. It is seen here passing New Bridge signalbox at 9.45am with a demonstration mixed freight bound for Pickering yard. (Author)

into use to protect the road crossing adjacent to the signalbox. These had been recommended after a Railway Inspectorate visit in 1972, and the work was financed by the County and District Councils as it was for their benefit and not an absolute requirement of the railway to provide this extra protection for what was officially only an occupation crossing.

Equally controversial was the provision of colour-light signals at Pickering a few years later. This decision had been made for purely operational reasons. The signalbox at High Mill crossing just north of Pickering had been demolished in 1970 but New Bridge signalbox a little further north had been listed as of historical importance by The Historic Buildings & Monuments Commission of England (English Heritage

after 1983) in November 1975. It was logical to re-use New Bridge for signalling purposes. British Rail had removed its eleven-lever, McKenzie & Holland frame and the wheel operating the gates before it closed the line, so the NYMR was able to make up a larger frame of twenty-one levers from McKenzie & Holland pattern parts and install this as well as a refurbished gate wheel. The re-signalling was planned as the new track layout was developed but it took some years to complete, between 1976 and full commissioning over the winter of 1985/86. As part of the work, High Mill became

The interior of New Bridge signalbox, Pickering, photographed in 2014. British Rail had removed the lever frame and all other instrumentation in 1965. The NYMR was not able to run trains into Pickering station until 1975, by which time all signalboxes there had been demolished. So the decision was taken to refit a lever frame into New Bridge to work new colour-light signals and electrically operated points between there and the station. The frame was made up of standard McKenzie & Holland components including a refurbished Samuel Dutton designed wheel to work the crossing gates. (Author)

The signalman at Goathland waits to collect the Grosmont Crossing–Goathland single line token from the fireman of 0-8-0 Class Q6 No. 63395 as it pulls into the station with the 5.15pm from Grosmont on 14 May 2016. The high visibility vest gives the twenty-first century footplate crew something to aim at. (Author)

The former NER signalbox at Grosmont photographed on 16 June 1960 when it still controlled the junction at the north end of the station. After closure it remained in situ until 25 March 1979 when the top (operating floor) section was removed to the station car park prior to its planned re-erection next to Front Street level crossing that never happened. (J.J. Davis)

an open crossing with flashing warning lights removing the need until then to employ a crossing keeper when trains were running.

By the 1980s, the NYMR had 'One Engine in Steam' in operation between New Bridge and Pickering station, 'Staff & Ticket' working between New Bridge and Levisham and between there and Goathland, with single line token working between Goathland and Grosmont Crossing using Tyers No. 6 tablet machines. The signalbox at the latter was a small hut next to Front Street level crossing, but it had been the intention to recommission the elevated signalbox at the north end of the station. To that end the signalbox interior had been cleaned in 1975 but then altered priorities halted any further work. With the focus then turned to a future extension of the platform, which would require British Rail to realign its track through the area

where the signalbox stood, the aim then became to resite it either adjacent to the road level crossing as an operational box, or on the platform as a museum piece. On 25 March 1979, the timber top (the operating room) was removed to the car park, and the remaining timber and brick base cleared away the following week. But again, priorities changed, funding was not available, and the plans were shelved. The operating room sat in the car park until October 1989 when it was dismantled and removed to Alston for possible reuse there.

Eventually, a completely new signalbox was erected immediately north-east of the level crossing at Grosmont using bricks recovered from Whitby Town's signalbox. The new structure was based on a NER Type SIa signalbox and was equipped with a fifty-two lever McKenzie & Holland frame and two gate wheels to work a reconfigured set

The NYMR-built signalbox adjacent to Front Street level crossing, based on a NER Type SIa (as classified by the Signalling Record Society in the 1970s), was commissioned for the May Bank Holiday in 1996, and photographed just a month short of the twentieth anniversary of that event in April 2016. (Author)

British Railways 4-6-0 Class 4MT No. 75029 entering Grosmont station from the south on 3 May 2014. The fabricated steel bracket supporting the upper quadrant semaphore signals on the right came from Whitby and was erected in its new position in the summer of 1989. Its partner on the left was salvaged from Consett and erected a little later that year. (Author)

Part of the metal lattice gantry from Falsgrave, Scarborough, supporting the semaphores controlling the north end of Grosmont station, photographed in April 2015. The signalling here was brought into use in July the previous year, improving access to and from the national rail network for NYMR trains working to and from Whitby. (Author)

The NER signals on the southern approach to Goathland station. The bracket was recovered from Glaisdale in January 1975 and craned into its new position on 2 October 1976. It was adapted to support the three signals needed to control the modified layout at Goathland necessitated by only a single track being retained between there and Levisham. The horizontal beams supporting the two shunting signals were replaced with new timber during the summer of 1990. The cast numbers screwed to the base of the post indicate which levers in the signalbox operate the three signals. (Author)

of crossing gates. It was brought into use along with a number of upper quadrant signals in May 1996 and won the Westinghouse Signalling Award in 2001. This impressive installation compensated in some way for the loss of the original Grosmont signalbox and the demolition in November 1994 of the remains of the signalbox at Newton Dale, which had long since been stripped of its lever frame and other equipment by British Rail. On a number of occasions it had been suggested that a passing loop should be laid at Newton Dale to break up the long single track section between Levisham and Goathland, but as the gradients where the box was located were not favourable, the loop would have had to be located elsewhere. The challenges of maintenance and security and the realities of manning such a remote signalbox with no operational purpose, sealed its fate.

On a more positive 'preservation' note, from the early 1970s, the NYMR had been actively collecting NER lower quadrant signals when British Rail were replacing them, and a number were salvaged and re-erected on the line. In 1974 the 25ft (7.6m) tall timber post with all its fittings was removed from Belmont Crossing, Harrogate. The following year, the post and cast-iron brackets from a signal at Glaisdale were salvaged and re-erected in a modified form to the south of Goathland station.

A further NER signal post and fittings were recovered by the York Group of the NYMR on 12 July 1977 from Wilstrop near Hammerton, where it was being replaced by a new distant signal. By the end of the 1970s, Levisham had seven operational authentic NER lower quadrant signals helping to balance out the comments of those who criticised the NYMR for installing modern colour-light signals at Pickering.

It is also interesting to compare the approach to the repair and replacement of these NER signals to that of permanent way. When the original posts and arms have had to be replaced because they were beyond repair, the purely practical, operational solution would have been to install upper quadrant semaphores on tubular metal posts, because they need less maintenance and spares are still readily available. The ultimate operational solution would have been to replace with colour-light signals! However, timber of the same proportions as the originals has been used and carefully formed to create replica NER signals. Obviously, this comparison has its limitations, but this author believes it is worth making.

Filming and Special Events

Many heritage railways have benefitted from being chosen by TV and film companies as shooting locations and the same has been true of the NYMR. For example, in 1992, £100,000 was earned from filming and passenger numbers were also given a considerable boost by the screening of what became one of television's classic series – 'Heartbeat'. Many locations in Goathland village, including the railway station, were used to create the fictional community of Aidensfield. The first episode was broadcast in 1992 and despite the Vice Chairman of the NYMR's subdued comment in 'Moors Line' for the summer of that year (No. 96) that 'The opening sequence each week shows a brief view of an NYMR train passing Fen Bog, and as some of the scenes show the Goathland area it may perhaps stimulate tourist interest', the series proved an instant and huge success. Before long, thousands of fans were making their pilgrimage to Goathland, and crowding onto NYMR trains.

For one dramatic episode broadcast in September 1993 involving a train crash,

NYMR timetable covers for the last five years of the twentieth century when the success of ITV's 'Heartbeat' series was helping to boost the NYMR passenger numbers and income to the levels experienced in the boom years of the late 1980s. (Author's collection)

a couple of carriages were strategically positioned outside Grosmont Tunnel to simulate the results of a derailment. The staging took place in January that year and in the following month one of the carefully damaged carriages was wrecked completely at Newton Dale Halt in a controlled explosion for the benefit of Central Television's 'Cook Report'. The purpose was to demonstrate the devastation that could be caused if a terrorist bomb exploded in a train. A useful £14,250 was made by the NYMR in fees from the TV companies and for the scrapping of the carriage.

Television and film work can be lucrative for the railway but it is not a guaranteed source of income. Since the 1980s what has become of major financial importance to the railway has been its regular and special events. Every year the NYMR stages themed days or weekends in order to attract return visitors. For railway enthusiasts, gala weekends are treated almost like annual pilgrimages, and for many families, Santa Specials are key to ensuring children's Christmas expectations are fulfilled. The increasing popularity of Halloween now rivalling Bonfire Night, has been of great benefit, dubious costumes and make-up being far less dangerous to stage than fireworks. In recent years the growing attraction of Second World War themed events has also provided another excuse for dressing up.

Hauling the 10.27am from Grosmont on 15 May 2016, the locomotive fireman obliges with a dramatic display of smoke for the photographers lined up at Darnholm just south of Goathland station. The 2-6-4T No. 80072 had been specially decked out as No. 80007, another member of its class, as part of the Scottish Branch Line Gala weekend, that latter locomotive having spent all its working life in Scotland at Polmadie and St Margaret's sheds. (Author)

Two former LNER A4 4-6-2s that entered service in the same year – 1937. No.4464 *Bittern* sports its 1930s Garter Blue livery, whilst behind, No. 60007 *Sir Nigel Gresley* (originally numbered 4498) is in early British Railways blue. Photographed at Grosmont during the 'Spring Steam Gala', May 2012. (Author)

On loan from the heritage Churnet Valley Railway, Baldwin Locomotive Company 2-8-0 No. 6046, built in 1945, double-heading with ex-LNER 4-6-0 Class B1 No. 61264 masquerading as another member of the same class, No. 61002, *Impala* on 5 October 2013 during the NYMR's 'LNER Weekend'. The two locomotives were making an easy, but noisy, job of climbing from Grosmont towards Beck Hole. (Author)

Showing no outward display of effort on the same stretch of line and on the same day as the Baldwin 2-8-0 and B1, ex-LNER 4-6-2 Class A4 No. 60007 *Sir Nigel Gresley* is hauling the dining train at Green End. (Author)

Whitby & Pickering Railway Revival

The surprisingly neat conclusion to this particular heritage railway story is that since 2007, regular passenger trains have been operated between Pickering and Whitby, reviving that railway service first introduced in 1836. It appears a logical achievement, but it has been both hard fought and controversial for the NYMR.

For a number of years after the Beeching cuts there was a period of paralysis throughout the British Rail network. Its trains and those of the NYMR ran into adjacent platforms at Grosmont station, but only the former were able to make the journey onwards to Whitby. Throughout the 1970s, Whitby Town station remained largely unaltered, with only the goods yard turned over for non-railway use. In 1972 the station buildings were designated Grade II on the list of historic buildings worthy of preservation, but then in the 1980s there was savage rationalisation. The line between Grosmont and Sleights had been reduced to a single track in 1972, but in 1984 the line between Sleights and

The 2pm departure from Whitby to Pickering photographed on 28 August 2014 from the A171 (Helredale Road) bridge with the River Esk to the left. (Author)

Whitby was also singled with only the former Platform 1 at Whitby remaining in use, with a section of the former up line retained as a sidings. The two signalboxes there (Bog Hall and Whitby) were closed.

Since the NYMR was formed, many people associated with that organisation had discussed whether or not running heritage trains into Whitby would be feasible some day. The severe cut-backs by British Rail in 1984 prompted more heart searching, and some believed the time was right to make Whitby the northern terminus of the NYMR by reinstating double track from Grosmont so that one line could be used exclusively for NYMR's trains. Ideas were aired for not only separate NYMR platforms at Whitby, but also engine and carriage sheds, and the reopening of the signalbox. If proof were needed that it was possible, then enthusiasts pointed to the SVR that had just extended to Kidderminster and was establishing an impressive terminus there, and to the Great Central Railway that was set to extend to a new railhead just north of Leicester. In November 1986, with the backing of Scarborough District Council and Whitby Town Council, it was decided to carry out a feasibility study into a possible extension of the NYMR. The Chairman of the NYMHRT felt any extension would over-stretch the resources of the railway, financially, in staffing levels and in motive power and rolling stock. When the report was published at the end of 1988 he must have been relieved to read it would indeed be operationally uneconomical to run to Whitby, although the social and economic benefits for the seaside town were felt to outweigh the problems. The report concluded that laying an extra track would be prohibitively expensive as British Rail had realigned its single track in many places, slewing the line across the former double-track formation. Axle loadings on bridges

was also highlighted as an issue. It was estimated the project would cost £2m. Another option of running steam trains over British Rail's single line was also considered uneconomical as British Rail required every train to be manned by its own staff and the pathing of trains run by an independent organisation was felt to be problematic.

British Rail did not want to invest in Whitby; it wanted to make money from the sale of its redundant land there, and in 1988 plans were submitted to Scarborough Borough Council for the building of a new supermarket on the site of Platforms 2, 3 and 4, with a new car park replacing the signalbox and remains of the goods shed. In 1990 a formal agreement was signed between the North Eastern Co-operative Society and the British Railways Board and work on clearing the site began. The NYMR was able to salvage 260 tons of facing stone and concrete coping slabs and was also given the option by the Co-op to dismantle Whitby signalbox as well. This was achieved during May and June 1990, leaving only the remains of the goods shed to be demolished by the contractors. The footprint of the new supermarket allowed just enough space for the reinstatement of a narrow Platform 2 in the future. Construction was rapid and the supermarket opened on 9 July 1991. Four months later, the 1847 engine shed with its 1868 extension immediately south of the station was listed Grade II by English Heritage to give that structure some protection from demolition.

As this relentless reduction in the railway infrastructure at Whitby added to inconvenient procedures necessary for through running between the NYMR and British Rail at Grosmont, it seemed the likelihood of a regular Whitby–Pickering service had been lost. Then came the privatisation of British Rail in 1994 and optimism returned, because that reorganisation brought with it the principle of open access, allowing any company to run their own trains almost anywhere on the national rail network provided they met certain operating standards. But the right to operate was still dependant on the state of the track and signalling, responsibility for which had passed from British Rail, firstly into the hands of Rail Track, and then to Network Rail. In 2003 the latter organisation assessed the track as too poor for the running of steam trains into Whitby by any operator.

Much lobbying followed and two years elapsed before the track was renewed. When that was completed, Network Rail allowed a limited steam-hauled service to be operated for the NYMR between Whitby and Glaisdale (with connections to the NYMR at Grosmont). The next step was for the NYMR to be allowed to run that service using its own footplate crews, and in January 2007 it became the first heritage railway to be granted a licence by the Office of the Rail Regulator to operate on the national rail network. With Network Rail support, the signalling at Grosmont was modified, and on 3 April 2007, the first NYMR service from Pickering ran to Whitby as the prelude to a regular service starting that Easter.

The 12.45pm departure from Whitby to Pickering on 28 August 2014 with Larpool Viaduct in the background. The footpath from which the photograph was taken was occupied by the up line until rationalisation in 1984. (Author)

Accelerating rapidly away from Grosmont on Saturday 14 May 2016 with the 2.46pm for Glaisdale, 2-6-0 No. 76079 had temporarily been given the number of an engine of the same class that had been based in Scotland. Other locomotives had similarly been renumbered as part of the NYMR's Scottish Branch Line Gala that month. (Author)

The increased mileage with all the attendant staffing issues and maintenance of engines and rolling stock to conform to the higher standards required to run on the national rail network, put a considerable strain on NYMR resources. Opinion was divided as to whether or not the effort was worth it. The 2008 season proved a challenge. Nevertheless, the NYMR management persevered and was given very positive support from all the organisations and local authorities involved in running and promoting the service. That level of support was such that within a few years all parties agreed to reinstate Platform 2 at Whitby. As two trains would then be able to occupy the station at the same time, this would not only improve operational flexibility if trains were running late but also enable more trains to be run by either the national operators (Northern Rail at the time) or the NYMR.

At the beginning of 2013, £1.1m was made available via the Government's Coastal Communities Fund, with a further £850,000 coming from Network Rail. Work started in February 2014 on both the platform and associated new trackwork, the former used by the first paying passengers on 12 August

B1 No. 61264 again with another change of identity as No. 61034 *Chiru* (an alternative name for the Tibetan gazelle), running around its train at Whitby on 28 August 2014. The new track and platform are very obvious, having been in use for NYMR trains for only sixteen days when this photograph was taken. If justification for the investment was needed, the train was packed. To the right is a small section of the Co-operative supermarket that was built over Platforms 3 and 4. (Author)

2014 before it was officially opened four days later. In parallel with this project was another to improve the signalling at the north end of Grosmont station. Fortuitously, the re-signalling of Scarborough station took place in 2010, and conveniently, the requirement for Network Rail to preserve the metal lattice signal gantry adjacent to Falsgrave signalbox because it was part of the latter's status of Grade II Listed, coincided with the NYMR's need for such a structure in its re-signalling at Grosmont. Network Rail could be relieved of its obligation to preserve by donating the gantry to the NYMR for 'preservation' at Grosmont. It went first to Invensis, the signalling contractor, at its Retford works for restoration, before being delivered to the NYMR in September 2012. By the end of that month, the shortened gantry had been re-erected at Grosmont with attention then focused on the timber signal posts (dolls) and all the relocking and electrical work necessary at Grosmont Crossing signalbox. The first stage of the project was completed at the beginning of July 2014 ready for the new Whitby service, and in the following year it was awarded the Siemens Signalling Award in the 2015 National Railway Heritage Awards, a fitting conclusion to this chapter, if not the whole story of the NYMR so far.

British Railways 2-6-0 Class 4MT No. 76079 bringing the 11.50am from Whitby into Grosmont's Platform 2 on 3 April 2016. It is passing the 'parachute' water column rescued from Derwenthaugh Junction near Gateshead and re-erected during 1990. Notice also the salvaged stone blocks used in 2003 when this platform was extended. (Author)

A view of the seven signals on the modified Falsgrave gantry at the north end of Grosmont station, brought into use in July 2014. The two main semaphores at the top the posts (or 'dolls') of equal height control entry on to the Esk Valley line (seen on the extreme left) from the NYMR's Platforms 2 and 3. The main semaphore on the right, on the shorter doll, is fixed at danger, indicating no train can pass from the NYMR's Platform 4 onto the Esk Valley line. All the smaller subsidiary or shunting signals beneath the three main arms control access to the sidings visible in the background. (Author)

Bibliography

The following is not a definitive list of all the books that have been written about the North Yorkshire Moors Railway, but a list of those used as references in the compilation of this book:

'Railways around Whitby', Martin Bairstow, published by the author, 1989

'The Scenery of the Whitby and Pickering Railway', H. Belcher, 1836

'An Illustrated History of the North Yorkshire Moors Railway', Philip Benham, OPC/Ian Allan Publishing, 2008

'North Yorkshire Moors Railway Stock Book 1990', N. Carter, North York Moors Historical Railway Trust, 1990

'Railways of the North York Moors', K. Hoole, Dalesman Books, 1983

'The North Yorkshire Moors Railway: a Past and Present Companion', John Hunt, Past & Present/The Nostalgia Collection, 2001

'Whitby and Pickering Railway', David Joy, Dalesman Books, 1973

'North Yorkshire Moors Railway: A Pictorial Survey', David Joy, Dalesman Books, 1991

'Guideline to the North Yorkshire Moors Railway', David Joy, North Yorkshire Moors Railway, 1998

'The North Eastern Railway, its Rise and Development', W.W. Tomlinson, Reid & Co., 1914

'North Yorkshire Moors Railway: A Pictorial Survey', Peter Williams & David Joy, Dalesman Books, 1977

'Official Opening by HRH The Duchess of Kent, May 1st 1973', souvenir booklet, 1973

Index

References to illustrations in **bold**